CHUCK GOETSCHEL

SIMON SAYS

Living your Life Purpose
...not just following the crowd

CHUCK GOETSCHEL

SIMON SAYS

Living your Life Purpose
...not just following the crowd

First Edition, February 2009

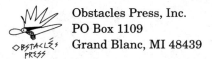 Obstacles Press, Inc.
PO Box 1109
Grand Blanc, MI 48439

Layout and design by Norm Williams
Cover Design by Lowell Norman

Printed in the United States of America

ACKNOWLEDGEMENTS

Writing a book is never an individual effort. While there are many people I would like to thank, that would require another book. However, I want to acknowledge some here.

First, I want to thank my family and close friends. It goes without saying that without their love and support, this book would not have been possible.

I would like to also acknowledge the numerous people who have participated in my blog surveys and discussions, attended my various speaking events, and suggested that I write a book. It was your questions and your encouragement that led to the creation of the final version you now hold in your hands. I hope that it serves you well.

I also wish to thank my various mentors, teachers and coaches. Specifically, Mike Troy — thank you for your years of coaching. You taught me well about work ethic, goal setting and persistence. Dan Williams, thank you for your many years of mentorship; your endless wisdom and humor taught me so much about life. Mom and Dad (Charlie & Betty), thank you for giving me a unique advantage in life by showing me a pure example of living with integrity and by sharing unconditional love and encouragement at all times.

Charlie Nickell, this book wouldn't be what it is without your help. Thank you for your creativity and all your manuscript editing. Greg Hardesty, thanks for your final review and input. Norm Williams, thanks for your patience and willingness to go the extra mile to complete the layout of this book. Lowell Norman, your work always is exceptional. Thanks for the book cover.

To everyone reading "Simon Says," I want to thank you and applaud you. Rather than drifting through life or worse, complaining that the world isn't devoting itself to making you happy, you are seeking God's true purpose for your life. Let me encourage you to join the "Simon Says" Revolution and encourage others to do the same.

Finally, let my greatest acknowledgement be to the one who has given each of us our Life Purpose to fulfill — our heavenly father above. I give Him all the credit and pray that this book brings people closer to Him.

SIMON SAYS

"SIMON Says…" We all played it as kids. When Simon said to do something, you did it. If you took action outside a "Simon says" command, you got busted to the elation of your friends who would jump up and down all the while pointing at you shouting, "Simon didn't say Simon says!" It was just a silly game. However, it wasn't meant to be played for the rest of your life!

Our world has an omnipresent voice that in many ways acts just like Simon dictating for most what they'll be thinking, feeling and doing for the rest of their lives. Are you still playing Simon says? Simon says "Grow up and act your age." Simon says "Collect as much stuff as you can." Simon says "Get a job, take an hour lunch, a two-week vacation and repeat that process for the next 45 years." Simon says, "Don't worry if your life doesn't fulfill your mind, body or soul." Simon says, "Keep in line and don't make waves, you'll be happy some day." Simon Says, "The perfect life isn't for you."

For just one moment let's forget what Simon says. What do you say? What does your heart tell you? What are your passions? What are your talents? You have been designed and created with a specific purpose that Simon doesn't care about. Stop playing the Simon Says game and start pursuing the life you were designed to live. Why are you still doing whatever Simon says?

Begin your inspired life today by joining others in a Simon Says Revolution! Be a part of the movement. Make a difference in your life and in the lives of others. Check out what it's all about at: www.SimonSaysRevolution.com

CONTENTS

A few years back, I was living a life that many would envy. I had achieved that which Simon would deem to be very successful. I had a family, financial independence and an amazing lifestyle. I worked hard for it. Then, in the blink of an eye, it all came crumbling down. I lost everything. I lost my family unit through divorce. I lost my business and my financial security through a conflict with partners over ethics and ideals. I lost most all semblance of my life and found myself facing the reality of my situation. I struggled greatly with my new reality.

I was no longer living in the gated community in my multimillion-dollar house on a championship golf course but rather a small, dark apartment with a handful of personal items. I was paying a furnishings company monthly rent for their "bachelor's package" which included generic kitchen necessities, an oak table, trash can, etc. I became so depressed, I would randomly cry throughout the day for no specific reason. I could hardly perform simple tasks like paying bills or maintaining a simple calendar. The details of even the smallest item overwhelmed me. I longed constantly to be with my two small boys; I never knew how much I could miss other human beings. In the still of night, everything seemed magnified as I would lay awake trying to maintain pace with the racing thoughts swirling inside of my head. Who am I? What really matters? How did I get here?

I remember asking myself, "How much lower can I go?" I

shouldn't have asked. I found out the answer when I decided to distract my loneliness by getting a dog. I went to an animal shelter and I was subsequently informed that I didn't qualify. I didn't qualify to adopt a stray dog! I remember asking the lady running the shelter, "Are you serious that I don't qualify to adopt that stray dog you found on the side of the freeway?!" "No sir, you don't." It seemed like just yesterday I was living the high life and now I didn't even qualify to adopt a stray dog. That was a sad realization (for both me and the dog).

Needless to say, God finally had my full attention. I began asking the right questions: What is life all about? What is my purpose here? What is His will for my life? Yes, these are the questions that a guy asked deep down inside a place he didn't know existed. I realized that it's not enough to apply success principles to your life. You must apply them to your God-given Life Purpose. For true inner peace, you must be in alignment with your creator's will for your life.

Although I don't wish my story on anyone, I can truly say that I am grateful for all that I have gained because of it. I feel a deep empathy with people and a love for people that I had never known before. I deeply care about people who are in pain, those who are lost, and even those who don't know they're lost. I have found my purpose. It is to be a leader, a teacher and an inspiration. And, in case you were wondering, I also now own a dog.

At some point during our life, each of us asks the question, "What is it all really about?" "Why am I here?" "What is the point?" There must be more to life than just working and surviving. Yes, there must be more to it. There must be hope for good; love and peace, meaning and purpose. And there is.

In fact, it's awaiting your discovery.

Your Life Purpose is specifically unique to you. You were designed for it. You have unique gifts, talents, passions and values that separate you from everyone else in the world. There is no other you. You are an original. The question is: Have you recognized these unique qualities and discovered how they are to be applied in your life? That is, are you living creatively on purpose or simply by accident?

Throughout this book, you will gain a new perspective of life. You will learn to stop playing Simon Says and start living *your* life. You will be lead through the discovery process of your Life Purpose which includes your purpose, your Personal Mission, and your Personal Assignment or calling. You will be taught the tools to empower you to pursue your purpose. And, you will be inspired to free yourself from the anchors of life allowing you to truly fulfill it.

I encourage you to begin a life of living on purpose. Enjoy!

It's All About the Dash

YOUR LIFE HAS A POINT

CHAPTER 1

Two of the Most Important Dates in Your Life

True happiness ... is not attained through self-gratification, but through fidelity to a worthy purpose.
–Helen Keller

> *Life's mission, therefore, is to discover, pursue and fulfill our Life Purpose.*

Your life has a point. It's been said that two of the most important dates in your life are the day you are born and the day you discover why you were born. Since we all know our birthday, the purpose of our life lies in discovering the answer to the more elusive second date. Life's mission, therefore, is to discover, pursue and fulfill our Life Purpose.

However, the challenge to living on purpose is that most people are programmed to do in life much in the same way we conditioned our thinking while playing the childhood game of Simon Says. Most played the silly game as kids and simply never broke the habit of following whatever Simon says. Yet, ultimately, when all is said and done, our life will be represented by a simple dash — that is, the dash between two dates: the day you were born and the day you die. At that time, the significance of your dash will be specifically measured by the success of your mission and not by how well you followed Simon's misguided directions. The point is, you have a Life Purpose. Discover it. Redesign your life to reflect it. Pursue

> *"If you aren't following your heart, then you're living someone else's dream."*

it and fulfill it. It's been said, "If you aren't following your heart, then you're living someone else's dream."

Each year we enjoy birthday celebrations (until we hit around 35). We go through great lengths to make birthdays a special day for our friends and family. And, we should! It is the day a special person in our life was born. A birthday is the one day each year we spotlight our individual existence, so to speak. Countless billions of dollars are spent each year on lavish birthday celebrations and we all gladly participate. So here's a thought: If two of the most important dates in your life are the day you are born and the day you discover why, then what if we also recognized the second date with at least as much enthusiasm as the first? That is, what if we recognized not just our 'Birth'-day but also our 'Purpose'-day? Our purpose day would be the specific day we discovered why we had a birthday. I know it sounds ridiculous, but it really shouldn't. Consider how much effort you actually played in your own birth. Would it be safe to say it wasn't a whole lot? In contrast, how much effort does it take to truly discover your purpose? I'd say even without your efforts, your birthday still happened. But, without your efforts, your purpose day could lay dormant and never arrive. Perhaps you're already living a life with clarity of purpose and seeking to fulfill it. If so, fantastic! Stay on it. However, perhaps you are not, and if you fall into this group, let this book be a launching point for you to initiate that quest of discovery.

A few years back (OK, maybe more than just a few) as an awed passenger in my proud friend's brand-new BMW, I discovered something intriguing. His shiny "Ultimate Driving Machine" was loaded with the latest technology but the most interesting feature within the electronic repertoire was an LCD screen displaying a digital map inset on what was at least for now a spotless dashboard.

"What's that?" I asked.

"It's my GPS," he said.

"Your GP what?" I asked, wondering why he was only teasing me with the cool acronym for his nifty device.

"It's a Global Positioning System," he said. "Satellites in space track my car and plot its exact location on a map on this screen."

At first, I thought he was kidding and I was subsequently slow to respond, worrying that I was about to be the brunt of a joke. However, something in the back of my mind was reminding me that I had heard about this new technology and so I responded with, "Can you connect with one of the satellites for me?"

"Absolutely!" he responded, full of new-ownership excitement. "First, you have to tell it where you want to go and then it can determine the course." After putting in our desired location, an arrow came onto the screen pointing in the direction we were supposed to precede. Then, suddenly, a voice began saying that it had calculated our best route and to proceed ahead.

"Your dashboard is talking to us," I said.

"Yep, and it will keep talking until we get there," he said.

Sure enough, the pleasant sounding "dashboard lady" continued her instructions: "In 500 feet turn right...at the next intersection make a left..."

I was amazed. "Is she always correct?" I asked.

"Yes, and if I miss a turn she is very patient. She'll just say, 'recalculating route' and then ask me to take an alternate path with no fuss."

"No fuss? I bet for most people, that takes some getting used to," I joked. "So if you don't put in a destination, what does she say?"

"Nothing," he said. "She can't help you if you don't have a destination."

And, so it is with life. Until you determine a destination, nobody knows if you're on course. Although a guiding voice is available, instructions aren't necessary because you really aren't traveling, you're wandering: You're a "wandering generality" instead of a "meaningful specific." Yes, I can hear you now, "I'm not wandering!" you may shout. Okay, then where are you going?

Let's consider the game of darts as an example. Even though one of the things I don't do a lot of is throwing darts, I am very confident that I could beat the World Champion Dart thrower if I could slightly modify the rules. Blindfold the champion, spin him/her in circles and then let's compete head to head. Do you think I may have an advantage? Do you think the champion may object, as they would be throwing darts in every direction? It certainly would draw a lot more spectators, making it more of a contact sport. However, come the end of the competition, regardless of how many darts the champion threw, I bet my experience would be much more pleasant and far more fruitful. "It's hard to hit a bulls eye when you don't have (or can't see) a target," I heard a wise man say once. Consequently, let's begin your journey to clearly define your target.

Your first step is to 'Stop!' Just stop for a moment. I know for many it can be a very difficult thing to do, but it is essential. For a few of you, this has never been a problem and we'll discuss the concept of 'Starting' later. But, for the majority, it is all about being very busy. Simon says, "Stay in motion; busy is good!" In fact, most people run through life in such a hurry they never stop and consider why it is they're in such a rush. "I don't really know where I'm going but at least I'm making great time!" would be an appropriate life slogan for many people. But, it has gone beyond just a fast pace. Our business has become some sort of new status symbol — a true source of misdirected pride.

"I'm very busy!" people constantly claim with a proud tone in their voice.

"Me too!" someone else will quickly chime in so as not to miss out on the mini-recognition ceremony taking place.

"I'm not" I love to contribute with a smile just to see them struggle to process the thought.

"You're not busy?" they begin questioning with a look of confusion and even a bit of concern.

"What is it that you do?" they ask.

"I play with my kids. I work out. I love to read..." I'll go on.

Inevitably they interrupt me, "That's not what I meant; what do you do for work?"

"Oh! Now that's a different question," I'll respond.

Most people are so busy working to make money that when asked, "What do you do?" they just assume the remaining part of the sentence is related to work, and consequently their entire identity has become their work title: "I'm an accountant," "I'm an attorney," "I'm a carpenter." You are? Is that who you ARE, or is that what you DO for a living?

It may seem like I'm splitting hairs here but I believe it is actually one of the sneaky traps that keep people from fulfilling their life purpose. Because we get caught up in the hustle and bustle of working, paying bills and generally getting through life our purpose is merely survival and our vehicle is our work. But, is your work in line with your purpose? Have you even thought about it? I mean *really* thought about it. Most people have not. It's like the guy visiting his neighbor only to see water covering the floor from a sink that's overflowing with a faucet still running. "Why don't you turn off the water?" the friend asks. "I don't have time to think about things like that. Can't you see I'm very busy trying to mop up this floor?" Yes, we are all very busy. We have this innate animalistic need to keep moving. But, remember, being busy doesn't necessarily mean being productive. Because you're in a hurry doesn't mean you are getting any closer to fulfilling your specific purpose. You will stop, sooner or later. We all will. If you stop now and think for a moment about your life, I'm certain your dash will represent so much more than it would have otherwise.

A second key to discovering your Life Purpose is to know where to look. Some people set off traveling around the world in search of answers. They may travel to the highest mountains and dive to the bottom of the deepest oceans in their quest but they will still be empty of purpose if they never look in the right place. Ironically, no matter where their travels take them, their answers travel with them. No, this discovery is not found outside but rather it is inside — inside of you revealed by your creator. Take a moment and point at yourself. Go ahead, no one is looking. Now, look at your finger. Is it pointing to your head? No, it isn't, is it? It's pointing to your heart. Who you ARE resides in your heart. Your Creator put it there. The process of this discovery is really a matter of connecting with what deep down you already know and asking God (your creator) for further clarification. Then, it's simply a matter of being open to God's will for your life (not Simon's will) as you travel along your journey.

CHAPTER 2

Every Birth Comes with a Purpose

Man's ideal state is realized when he has fulfilled the purpose for which he is born. And what is it that reason demands of him? Something very easy—that he live in accordance with his own nature.
—*Seneca*

Discovering your Life Purpose is exciting and obviously life transforming. Unfortunately, most people have a hard time believing that their life could have any real particular purpose.

> *Unfortunately, most people have a hard time believing that their life could have any real particular purpose.*

A young boy was removed from his mother's care because of severe abuse. She was a drug addicted prostitute whose customers had sexually abused him. His mother intentionally burned him once by justifying she had to punish him because he was a "bad boy" for scaring off a potential customer. As difficult as it may be for this boy to believe, he has a unique Life Purpose.

A young woman in her late 20s recently commented in an Internet chat room, "It's hard to figure out what I am supposed to do next. I feel like I'm floating through life aimlessly, and the days are just blurring together. Sometimes, when people ask what I did last week, I honestly have no clue. We are all waiting for that special something that tells us our place in the universe so that we can be fulfilled and know true happiness. Well, how long does it take? How can I get to it? What do I need to do to get pointed in the right direction?" As difficult as it may be for this woman to discover, she has a unique Life Purpose.

A successful businessman in his late 40s starts to awaken to his reality. He has built a very large and profitable business. By the world's standards, he is very successful. Yet, he's empty inside. He finds himself feeling anxious as he recognizes that his work consumes his life; work that he is not even passionate about. "What is it all for anyway?" he wonders. He feels trapped as his family's lifestyle is supported by his business. "There is no way out," he concludes and slowly slips into a quiet depression. As difficult as it may be for this businessman to acknowledge, he has a Life Purpose and he's not living it. It is time for him to responsibly begin the journey.

If you have been born, then you have a Life Purpose. Remember, that is in fact the reason why you were born in the first place!

"I was just an accident" I have heard many times.

"How do you know?" I always ask.

"My parents told me..." is typically the response.

Friends, nobody is an accident. Your life is not an accident. As Rick Warren, author of "The Purpose-Driven Life," has said, "There are accidental parents. There are no accidental children. There are illegitimate parents. There are no illegitimate children. Your parents may not have planned you but God planned you. Really it doesn't matter whether your parents were good, bad, or indifferent. They may have even abandoned you. But they were the parents God chose for you. Why? Because they had just the right DNA to create you. And God was more interested in making you than He was in their parenting skills." Interestingly, Pope Clement VII, Leonardo da Vinci, Alexander Hamilton and even Josephine de Beauharnais (Napoleon's wife) have something in common...they were all born of illegitimate parents.

Once you understand that you were uniquely designed to be just who you are, then it would make sense that you would have a specific purpose. Think about it: What object has ever been uniquely designed and produced without purpose in mind for it? The automobile was designed and produced to help people travel faster, farther and in comfort. The telephone was designed and produced to increase our ability to communicate. Preparation H was designed and produced for puffy eyes. Just kidding...not totally.

> *The bottom line is that nothing was designed and produced without value and a purpose.*

But, you get the point. Everything is designed and produced for a specific purpose and often, such as my last example, it may have related and surprisingly additional purposes to its original primary intent. The bottom line is that nothing was designed and produced without value and a purpose. Most importantly is that you grasp *your* value and purpose rather than simply doing whatever Simon says.

In contrast, everything produced can also be used in activities that are not in line with their purpose. I was 5 years old when my parents purchased new bedroom furniture. Somehow I ended up with a hammer in my bedroom during nap time and decided to add my own personal touch to their new furniture. It was fun until my mom showed up. I don't know which had the more "distressed look" — my dresser or my mom. I quickly learned from her that the hammer was not designed and produced to destroy new bedroom furniture even though it was quite effective. How many people on this planet are acting the same way — using their gifts to destroy rather than to build?

Adolf Hitler is considered one of the world's greatest leaders. That may come as a surprise to you but it is indisputably true. In fact, in 1938, Time Magazine awarded him "Person of the Year." Dreadfully, he ended up being a leader of evil and not good. John Maxwell's "21 Irrefutable Laws of Leadership" defines leadership as "influence — nothing more, nothing less." Peter Drucker's forward to "The Leader of the Future" sums up leadership: "The only definition of a leader is someone who has followers." Adolf Hitler had tremendous influence and was followed by an army of people. Tragically, his influence led to some of the most horrific acts ever committed against humanity. It is reported that Hitler killed 11 million people. About 6 million Jews and 5 million other people of different ethnic origins were killed in concentration camps. This is not counting the thousands killed by German soldiers in Russia and Western Europe. Imagine if he had used his ability to influence people for good instead of evil. What enormous positive impact could have resulted?

There is a fable that tells of a man who dies and is met by an angel. He is shown two rooms. In the first room, he sees a full display of his life. He sees the people in his life and the many events that took place. He watches all that he did and the effects that it had on other people. It was emotional and it was telling of what his life was all about. Next, he was shown the second room. In the second room he saw some people that he recognized but many that he didn't. He saw events that weren't familiar but beautiful. He saw people's lives in a much better place than they were in the first room. It was confusing and a bit disturbing as he wished that those events had actually happened in his life. When he asked what the second room was all about, he was told, "The first room was your life as it was and the second room was your life as it was meant to be had you fulfilled your life purpose."

In 1940, just two years after Time Magazine named Adolf Hitler "Person of the Year," Winston Churchill was given the same honor. Winston Churchill, in obvious contrast, used his leadership abilities for good. When he was 66 years old he became prime minister of Great Britain. His role in WWII is historic. His fiery resolve to resist, his inspiring speeches, and diplomatic and military initiatives not only affected Great Britain but also, unarguably, impacted the world. He said, "I felt as if I were walking with destiny, and that all my past life had been but a preparation for this hour and for this trial". Imagine 66 years of preparation in order to have the character and wisdom to fulfill your life mission. The world is obviously a very different place thanks to his resolve and his "walking with destiny." Most appropriately, it was Churchill and not Hitler who in 1949 Time Magazine named "Man of the Half-Century."

CHAPTER 3

The Three Levels of Living

It is not length of life, but depth of life.
–Ralph Waldo Emerson

I was a wet-behind-the-ears 25-year-old when first sitting at a restaurant with a new financial mentor of mine, Dan Williams, as he explained the three levels of living. "The first level is survival. Most people find themselves just treading water.

> *The three levels of living: Survival, Success, Significance.*

Their life is full of stress," he explained. I understood it well at the time. I was single, broke, living in a one-bedroom condominium, and driving the coveted 1982 Dodge colt with a leaky sunroof. "Many of us start off in survival mode," he said, probably noticing my slight discomfort. "Unfortunately, many people will stay there forever; time-starved, stressed, hurrying, living paycheck to paycheck, and dreaming of the second level although it seems unattainable."

The second level is success. Everyone has a different picture of what "success" looks like. But for everyone it's a step past survival. We all want to be successful. I have yet to meet someone who has told me that they are just trying to fail on a more consistent basis. Unfortunately, people often strive for success as it is their sincere hope for happiness. *I'll finally be happy when I get that promotion...when we own our own home...when we can travel to Hawaii...* Yet, although happiness can result momentarily from those things, they will never produce long-lasting deep happiness and joy. Don't get me wrong; I have nothing against financial success. Although money doesn't buy happiness, neither does poverty. Money is a tool that can be used to hurt or help. It can provide comfort or cause concern. Money is neither good nor bad. I have yet to see a $20 bill leap off the counter and slap someone upside the head. If it were bad, Satan would be doubling your income every day. However, true happiness and ultimately deep joy comes from discovering, pursuing and fulfilling your Life Purpose.

> *Money is neither good nor bad. I have yet to see a $20 bill leap off the counter and slap someone upside the head.*

The third level of living is significance. Unlike survival or success, living a purpose-driven, significant life will yield a fulfilling sense of peace and pleasure. As my mentor Dan was finishing his explanation, he slid his glass of water across the linen-covered dining table to its center. He then put his finger in it, took it out, looked at me and asked, "What changed?" All I could think at the time was that, "Now it's dirty" although I figured that wasn't the right answer and simply responded with, "Nothing." "Exactly," he said. "That is exactly how most people live their life. They enter the world, hang out for a while, and then depart without a trace of their ever having been there. Not even a ripple of effect. Don't live that way. Strive for significance by making waves and creating a difference in the lives of others." Survival. Success. Significance.

The more I pondered the concept of living a life of significance, the more I was brought back in time by a memory of my Great Uncle George. My father's uncle was named George Gaude. He was a part of the Normandy D-Day invasion of WWII. In fact, he was in one of the early waves landing on the beachfront via a rugged Higgins assault boat. He knew his odds of survival were slim. A good friend of his, also in an early wave, wrote his parents a letter just before the invasion expressing his love to them and his gratitude for their love. He requested that they honor him with a sense of pride, as he most likely would not be returning from this one-sided engagement. As a parent myself, I could only imagine the emotions I would feel reading such a letter from my own son.

The morning came and my Great Uncle George found himself amongst a number of other brave soldiers packed like sardines in a Higgins boat. The boat bottomed out in shallow water and everyone attempted to scramble out without being shot. He made it. As he ditched the boat and submerged into the frigid ocean water, he and everyone else attempted to get out without being shot or drowning from the sheer weight of their gear. He made it out and onto the beach. Amidst the raining down of bullets, exploding mines and mortars, he ran up the beach. Amazingly, he made it across the beach to the hillside. However, it was here where he was hit by a mortar ripping off part of his leg and sending shrapnel throughout his entire body. Like a rag doll, he spun around and fell on his back. With continuing bullets flying everywhere, explosions and general chaos in all directions, my Great Uncle George lay on the upper beach, blood pouring out from his body. At that moment, he pulled out a picture of his family and held it tightly on his chest with his bloody hands. He held it tightly until he passed out. We know this because when the medics came for him the following morning, he still had it clutched to his chest. After all, wasn't it for his family that he was laying on that beach giving his life so others could freely live theirs?

Well, when the medics did pick him up, it is recorded that they yelled, "This one's not cold! He's still alive!" Somehow, through it all, he had not bled to death. And, long story short, operation after operation, he lived! He lived to the point that when I was a small boy he told me this story himself. He showed me his reconstructed leg that was now several inches shorter than the other. He showed me the remaining shrapnel that could still be seen just under his skin. He told me about lying on his back holding the picture of his family he was certain he'd never see again. He told me all about it. Then, he looked at me and told me how his good friend and many others never did make it off that beach. He told me how the only way to give their deaths significance was not to take our freedom for granted. "Do something great with your life!" he told me.

CHAPTER 4

Title or Testimony?

Make your work to be in keeping with your purpose.
–Leonardo da Vinci

Anthony Campolo is a popular Christian author and speaker who offers some challenging insight for examining our lives. At the time of our death, he writes, "We will be remembered for either our titles or our testimonies." There are those individuals who will be remembered for their titles: vice president of the company, head of the Yacht Club, coach of the youth team, chairman of the fundraiser. On the other hand, there will be those who will be remembered for the testimonies of their service to others. The person who positively impacts the life of another in a spiritual fashion leaves a testimony. In leaving a testimony, we have marked another person's life because God has used us to make a difference.

Campolo makes his point as he retells a sermon by his pastor: "You're all gonna die. You can live for a title or a testimony. Pharaoh had a title but Moses had a testimony. Ahab had a title but Elijah had a testimony. Nebuchadnezzar had a title but Daniel had a testimony. Pilate had a title but my Lord Jesus Christ had a testimony." It is true. There will come a day when your time on earth will come to an end. People you know will gather around, eat some potato salad and talk about you. What are they going to be talking about? "Boy, Bill sure had a cool job." "Mary was the CEO of which Fortune 500 Company?" Of course there's nothing wrong with a good title but let's hope they are talking about your testimony. Yes, your title may afford you some nice things, but let's face it: until the day comes where I see a hearse pulling a U-Haul, I don't believe you take it with you. If it were tomorrow, would they be talking about your title or talking about your testimony? Sobering thought, isn't it? If so, don't put the book down, it gets better. There are only three reasons why that discussion won't be about your testimony and, once you understand them, the responsibility is all yours.

The first reason people die without a testimony is ignorance. Now, don't confuse that with stupidity. Ignorance is simply the condition of being uneducated, unaware or uninformed. Stupidity is well...as Webster bluntly puts it: the quality or condition of being stupid. Most people are just too busy to get educated. We find ourselves in this apparent race — with whom or what nobody really knows...don't even have time to think about that! We must hurry and climb the corporate ladder. We rush our infants to daycare and kids to school and practice. We race to the grocery store to get food for dinner. Oh no, the bills are late! What do you mean the engine light came on in the car? Why sure, we'd love for you to come and visit. As a friend said to me once, "I'm wiped out — I feel like a bug on the windshield of life." In the midst of our fast-paced, chaotic lives and while virtually trying not to feel splattered on the windshield of some passing bus of life, I can understand why it doesn't seem fitting to stop and ponder the meaning of our life. However, our craziness should not be our excuse as to why we stay ignorant — rather, it should be our reason to question. You may have heard the definition of insanity is doing the same thing over and over expecting a different result. If we want a change in our life, we need to make...well, a change in our life. Deep, isn't it? It really is.

Some people aren't too busy to get educated but simply believe that they don't need to learn. Unfortunately, these people aren't just ignorant, they are also arrogant. Fun people to be around. Not really. Ever hear of a know-it-all? They are either telling you about their success or informing you how you could be doing better or both. It's hard for them to learn anything new when they are always the one giving the advice. As the saying goes, "God gave you two ears and one mouth — it's best when you use them proportionately." Similarly, as my financial mentor Dan Williams said to me once I finally started seeking his advice, "I knew once you hit your head against the wall long enough, your ears would pop out." Funny man, but he was right.

> *"God gave you two ears and one mouth-- it's best when you use them proportionately."*

There are always plenty of lessons to learn as we travel through life. Notice particularly the last lesson at age 92 in the following list. The sooner we learn that one, the better! Most importantly, let's learn the truth that life is really all about our mission — producing a testimony that fulfills our life purpose.

I've Learned

I've learned that you can't hide a piece of broccoli
in a glass of milk. Age 6

I've learned that just when I get my room the way I like it,
Mom makes me clean it up. Age 12

I've learned that although it's hard to admit it, I'm secretly
glad my parents are strict with me. Age 15

I've learned that silent company is often more healing than
words of advice. Age 24

I've learned...that if someone says something unkind about
me, I must live so that no one will believe it. Age 39

I've learned that the greater a person's sense of guilt, the
greater his need to cast blame on others. Age 45

I've learned that children and grandparents
are natural allies. Age 46

I've learned that singing "Amazing Grace" can lift
my spirits for hours. Age 49

I've learned that motel mattresses are better on the side
away from the phone. Age 50

I've learned that you can tell a lot about a man by the way
he handles these three things: a rainy day, lost luggage, and
tangled Christmas tree lights. Age 52

I've learned that regardless of your relationship with your parents, you miss them terribly after they die. Age 53

I've learned that making a living is not the same thing as making a life. Age 55

I've learned that life sometimes gives you a second chance. Age 62

I've learned that whenever I decide something with kindness, I usually make the right decision. Age 66

I've learned that everyone can use a prayer. Age 72

I've learned that it pays to believe in miracles. And to tell the truth, I've seen several. Age 73

I've learned that even when I have pains, I don't have to be one. Age 82

I've learned that every day you should reach out and touch someone. People love that human touch — holding hands, a warm hug, or just a friendly pat on the back. Age 85

I've learned that I still have a lot to learn. Age 92

-Anonymous

The second reason people die without a testimony is excuses. There is a saying that, "Those who say it can't be done are regularly interrupted by those who are doing it." With an awareness that this may read insensitively, understand it is time to excuse your excuses! You can hang on to them and let merely age be your defining change, or you can excuse them and move on with your life's mission. Please don't misunderstand. I sympathize and even empathize with many experiences people have had that has caused them to stop dead in their tracks in this thing called life. In fact, it is the pain that I feel for a person that has lead me to pursue my mission with great passion. Here is some tough love: I believe for every excuse you have that is stopping you from pursuing your mission, there is someone else with the same or worse scenario who is busy doing it. It really isn't that you are too old or too young, too uneducated or too knowledgeable, too introverted or too outgoing, that you had too difficult of a childhood or too perfect of one, too this or too that. It is simply something you are allowing to hold you back while someone else is moving forward in spite of it. So, if you do choose to stick with your excuses then at least pick a good one and stick with it. Don't flip-flop all around; it messes up your story. After all, since you aren't going to have a testimony that inspires others, at least you have a consistent sad story to tell. Again, I don't mean to be insensitive but, really, don't you think it is time to excuse your excuses and move on with your life?

> *I believe for every excuse you have that is stopping you from pursuing your mission, there is someone else with the same or worse scenario who is busy doing it.*

The third reason people die without a testimony is fear.

Fear is more than an excuse. An excuse is a cognitive reason for not doing something. Fear, on the other hand, is an emotional response to perceived impending danger and varies extremely in degree from mild caution to extreme phobia and paranoia. Some fear can be healthy. A close friend of mine spoke about his fear that caused the additional alertness that was essential to keeping him alive during his tours in Vietnam. However, most of us are not literally in a battle being shot at and our fear is on a different level. For us, the challenge is twofold. First, most of our fears never materialize and we find ourselves worrying over nothing. This issue supports the saying that FEAR is just "False Evidence Appearing Real." The second issue with fear is that we are looking only to our self for our success. Subscribe to the philosophy, "Work like it all depends upon you. Pray like it all depends upon God."

> *"Work like it all depends upon you. Pray like it all depends upon God."*

I was going through a difficult time and apparently my anxiety was showing (oops...how embarrassing). I knew this because my dad asked me if he could talk to me about it. My dad is a unique person. He has many amazing qualities and one of them is that he never worries. He has incredible faith. He looked at me and said, "I've noticed that you are getting more and more anxious. Either you believe that God has a plan for your life or He doesn't. Your anxiety is exposing your lack of faith that He does have a plan for you." Wow...that was a powerful punch. It's true — either you believe He has a plan

> *"Either you believe that God has a plan for your life or He doesn't. Your anxiety is exposing your lack of faith that He does have a plan for you."*
> *--Charlie Goetschel*

for you or you don't. And, if you don't, let me refer you back to my first reason people die without a testimony and challenge you to gain more knowledge. After all, the whole point here is that there is a plan and purpose for your life. Rick Warren says, "When God is not at the center of your life, it can be seen by the sign of 'worry'. Anything more important than God will become a source of worry. You can pray or panic. You can worry or worship."

Why worry about tomorrow?

Why worry about tomorrow, shall I stew about it now?
Shall I say, It is no use, give it up, throw in the towel?
Why worry about tomorrow, will it bring me health and gain?
Or shall I wake up in the morning, in poverty and pain?
Why worry about tomorrow, whatever comes my way?
I've got all that I can handle just to make it through today.
Why worry about tomorrow? There's no point or so it seems.
Will I wake up in the morning and find it's all been just a dream?
Tomorrow is only maybe, and though yesterday was rough.
Today is all I have, and yes, today is quite enough.
Yes, it's fun to dream, and there is nothing wrong with hopes.
But there's still a Master Planner, and He may just tell us Nope.
There is One who holds tomorrow, and only He knows what is best.
So I'll place my hand in His, He will help me meet the test.
I can't worry about tomorrow, it is God's and God's alone.
For today, I'll do my best, and give thanks when it is gone.

© 1999, Jerry Ham

CHAPTER 5

You are a Solution to Someone

The greatest good you can do for another is not just to share your riches but to reveal to him his own.
—Benjamin Disraeli

Somebody needs you. Whether you realize it or want to believe it or not, your mission in life will be connected with somebody else. There is some person or persons whom you are to effect. Often, it seems impossible that you

> *Whether you realize it or want to believe it or not, your mission in life will be connected with somebody else.*

could individually ever make a significant contribution or have a meaningful life purpose but remember, your actions will send into motion a ripple effect that may well transcend more than you could ever imagine. Consequently, does your purpose need to be huge to be worthy? Not at all. As Rick Warren says, "Never confuse prominence with significance. You may not be prominent but you are still significant." Your 'simple' purpose can be priceless to someone else.

Consider Norman Ernest Borlaug. He is often credited with saving over a billion people from starvation and was awarded the Nobel Peace Prize in 1970 in recognition of his contributions to world peace through increased food supply. He took up an agricultural research position in Mexico where he developed disease-resistant, high-yielding wheat. He then combined these high-yielding varieties with modern agricultural production techniques and introduced them to Mexico, Pakistan and India. The result dramatically increased food security in those nations. The work of Borlaug and others in expanding yields of corn, wheat and rice prevented worldwide famine.

So, although Norman Ernest Borlaug receives the credit for saving over a billion people from starvation, I suggest you also consider Henry Wallace. In 1933, Henry Wallace became America's Secretary of Agriculture under President Franklin Roosevelt. Then in 1940, he became vice president under Roosevelt. After the 1940 election he went on a vacation to Mexico. While he was there he noticed that although corn was a very important part of the Mexican diet, their yield was very low compared to America. Consequently, upon his return home, he created experimental stations in Mexico to develop improved corn varieties. Borlaug was one of the first scientists to join the station started by Wallace. So, perhaps credit for saving over a billion people should go to Henry Wallace for establishing the stations in Mexico where Borlaug did his research.

Or, perhaps, you should consider George Washington Carver. George Washington Carver became one of the nation's greatest educators and agricultural researchers. Carver discovered 300 uses for peanuts and hundreds more uses for soybeans, pecans and sweet potatoes. Carver attended Iowa State University and used to take long walks into the surrounding fields to study plants for research. On some of these walks he took a little friend with him. His friend was the 6-year-old son of a dairy science professor. Carver shared his love of plants, and the boy responded enthusiastically. At the age of 11, that boy began doing experiments with different varieties of corn. His name was Henry A. Wallace. So, perhaps credit for saving over a billion people should go to George Washington Carver for having significant influence over Henry Wallace who established the stations in Mexico where Borlaug did his research.

Or, perhaps, you should consider Etta May Budd. Etta May Budd taught art at Simpson College in Indianola. There she met a young man who was enrolled in one of her art classes. He loved to paint, especially still-life paintings of plants and flowers. He also was a good gardener and Etta Budd helped him find gardening jobs with families in the area. She took the young man aside one day and urged him to study something besides art — instead of painting plants, she encouraged him to study them. She offered to go with him to Iowa State where her father was a professor. After thinking about it, the young man, George Washington Carver, agreed to enroll at Iowa State. So, perhaps credit for saving over a billion people should go to Etta Budd for influencing George Washington Carver to attend Iowa State where he would meet and influence Henry Wallace who established the stations in Mexico where Borlaug did his research.

Or perhaps, you should consider a German farmer back in the 1860s during the American Civil War. Night riders kidnapped a slave mother and her sickly infant baby boy from the farmer. The farmer then offered a neighbor his fastest racehorse for their return. The neighbor agreed but returned with only the sickly boy as the mother had died. The farmer and his wife raised and educated this boy as if he was their own. The boy: George Washington Carver. The farmer and his wife: Moses and Susan Carver. So, perhaps credit for saving over a billion people should go to Moses and Susan Carver for trading their best racehorse to save the life of George Washington Carver who would be influenced by Etta Budd to attend Iowa State where he would meet and influence Henry Wallace who established the stations in Mexico where Borlaug did his research.

Or, perhaps…well, you get the point.

You never know how big of an impact your life may have on others (perhaps billions of people) since you never how what "ripples" will continue from the effect your life had on another. Consequently, the apparent size of your mission is not what's important. Rather, what is important is that you are seeking to discover, pursue and fulfill your Life Purpose no matter how small or how large it may appear.

The Star Thrower

Once upon a time, there was a wise man who used to go to the ocean to do his writing. He had a habit of walking on the beach before he began his work.

One day, as he was walking along the shore, he looked down the beach and saw a human figure moving like a dancer. He smiled to himself at the thought of someone who would dance to the day, and so, he walked faster to catch up.

As he got closer, he noticed that the figure was that of a young man, and that what he was doing was not dancing at all. The young man was reaching down to the shore, picking up small objects, and throwing them into the ocean.

He came closer still and called out "Good morning! May I ask what it is that you are doing?"

The young man paused, looked up, and replied. "Throwing starfish into the ocean."

"I must ask, then, why are you throwing starfish into the ocean?" asked the somewhat startled wise man.

To this, the young man replied, "The sun is up and the tide is going out. If I don't throw them in, they'll die."

Upon hearing this, the wise man commented, "But, young man, do you not realize that there are miles and miles of beach and there are starfish all along every mile? You can't possibly make a difference!"

At this, the young man bent down, picked up yet another starfish, and threw it into the ocean. As it met the water, he said, "It made a difference for that one."

-Loren Eiseley

Section 2

Discovering Your Life Purpose

THE DISCOVERY PROCESS.

CHAPTER 6

It's not a Decision,
it's a Discovery

*The greatest explorer on this earth never takes
voyages as long as those of the man who descends to
the depth of his heart.*
—Julien Green

There are certainly some things that we "decide" in our life but your Life Purpose is not one of those things. Certainly, many of your decisions will be a direct result of your Life Purpose, but your purpose itself must be discovered. This is why so many people miss it. It's hard to discover much of anything when you're continuously racing at 100 miles per hour playing the Simon Says game. One of the reasons I love children so much is that they're permanently in the non-stop discovery mode. They haven't developed the bad habit of racing by everything like most adults. They are curious. They will explore. They will admire what most would not even notice. In fact, to them the world is really just one great big playground filled with surprises everywhere to be discovered.

The other day, I was walking alongside my 4-year-old son. He was riding his bicycle and loving it! He rode one big loop, returned to the house for a quick run to the bathroom and then decided he wanted to ride to the park. I calculated that it would be nearly three total miles of cycling for him. It seemed like a lot to me for a 4-year-old but he didn't want to hear my concerns and began his trek to the park. He rode and rode, continually saying, "I'm fast and strong. Can you see it [the park] yet Daddy?" About ½ a mile from the park, he stopped. "What are you doing?" I asked. "Look Daddy! Look at this puddle!" He was full of excitement as he got off his bicycle and sat down next to the puddle. He pointed out to me everything in it...the leaves, the stones, and even the miscellaneous, unidentifiable stuff. The morning sun was reflecting off of it and the more I looked at it, the more beautiful I realized it really was. Strange, in the midst of so much chaos in the world and plenty of goings-on in my own life, I found myself admiring the beauty of a random puddle. It was calming. "It's beautiful," I said to him. "God made it just for us," my son instantly replied. "He made it just for you and me?" I asked. "You, me, Lightning McQueen and Dynaco King," he said, including his two favorite characters from the Pixar movie "Cars." With that, he jumped back onto his bicycle and completed his journey to the park, dramatically picking up his pace as soon as the swings came into view.

> *Don't let the drama of the world and the challenges in your own life keep you from admiring God's beauty.*

So, what does this story have to do with your Life Purpose? First, don't let anyone put limitations on what you can achieve. Conversely, don't put limitations on others. Beware, it may even be your "Daddy" meaning well by trying to "protect" you. Yes, you may have more natural talents in some areas and more limitations in others, but you be the one to discover what those actually are. Second, don't let the drama of the world and the challenges in your own life keep you from admiring God's beauty. The process of discovering your Life Purpose begins with slowing down enough to allow some of the little things in life to grab your attention. Critical people and challenging times need not grab your attention from the joy even a puddle can provide. Finally, keep your sights on where you are going. Keep in mind the purpose of your mission. And know that when you really can "see it," you'll discover that you have all the energy in the world to finish strong.

Part of the process of discovering your Life Purpose has to do with being in touch with your feelings. (Guys, don't close the book!) Your feelings are clues to what your life purpose is all about. By noticing how you feel about things, you'll discover what you value and what you don't. Things that don't trigger much emotion probably aren't tied to your purpose or the application of it — at least for now. Things that you become emotional over may well be connected. Many of us, guys particularly, have a hard time "getting in touch" with ourselves this way. It sounds dangerous and many don't naturally go there. I was first introduced to this by a simple dialog one day with a relationship mentor of mine. It went like this:

"How are you feeling?" he asked me.

"Great!" I responded enthusiastically.

"You didn't answer my question," he said.

"I'm great," I repeated.

"It's a simple question — can you just answer it for me?" he continued.

"I was great but now I'm just OK," I somewhat sarcastically responded, not knowing where he was going with this.

"Are you afraid of confronting the truth?" he added.

"Do you know something I don't?" I asked, now completely confused.

"Well, yes. I know that when I asked you how you were *feeling* all you could do is tell me how you were *doing*. You're doing 'Great', you're doing 'OK'. Wonderful, but I didn't ask you how you were *doing*. I asked you, 'How are you *feeling?*'"

"OK. Right now I'm feeling frustrated."

"Fantastic!" he exclaimed. "Why didn't you just share that from the beginning?!"

Have you ever had one of those moments where your brain started overheating? This was one of those moments for me. "What is he talking about? And, why is he playing with my mind," I was thinking. "Don't play with your food!" I told him, giving a subtle reference of his mental superiority at the moment. However, the more he explained how really out of touch we are with our daily feelings and, consequently, how unaware we are of things that matter to us, the more it made sense to me. Being aware of your feelings will give you great insights as to what you value. Our feelings are like a gauge on the driver's dash. When the needle moves, something relevant is happening and it makes sense to take note of it. "How do you feel about this?" he asked. "What about this? How did you feel when you saw that?" he continued. For each question I searched how I felt and was amazed. I was literally discovering things about myself that were obviously meaningful to me that I had never even realized before.

> *Ultimately, our strongest feelings direct us towards our Personal Assignment or calling.*

Ultimately, our strongest feelings direct us towards our Personal Assignment, or calling. We have been given a specific purpose that is designed to affect all areas of our life. However, there is one area of life that contains a problem that our unique purpose and abilities are designed to solve. Solving this problem is our Personal Assignment — our calling. As Stephen Covey writes in *The 8th Habit,* "When you engage in a work that taps your talent and fuels your passion—that rises out of a great need in the world that you feel drawn by conscience to meet—therein lies your voice, your calling, your soul's code.

CHAPTER 7

What You Love Most is a Clue to Your Personal Assignment

*Doing what you love is the cornerstone of
having abundance in your life.*
–Wayne Dyer

What is it that you love to do? What do you enjoy doing that brings you peace and happiness? If you could only
do one thing and you were assured to find success doing it,
what would it be? We all have personal interests typically
with aligning gifts and talents that we may or may not be
pursuing. For most of us, we grew up thinking that what we
loved to do and what we actually should do were almost certainly two different things. Consequently, we charged down
life pursuing that which we believed we should do only to
find ourselves tired and stressed. In a survey I performed
with hundreds of people from a variety of backgrounds, only
15% said they did what they did for an occupation because
they knew it was what they were designed to do. The remaining 85% of the people had reasons other than doing it
because they loved it and were designed for it — such as it

was the highest-paying opportunity, the most flexible hours, or simply the only thing that they could find to do. Interestingly, in another survey done with the same people, when asked which emotion they felt most often, "Stress" was the No. 1 answer. Following what Simon says we should do, rather than following our heart, doesn't lead us to peace, joy and happiness. As the saying goes, "Find something you love doing, and you'll retire for the rest of your life."

> *Following what Simon says we should do rather than following our heart, doesn't lead us to peace, joy, and happiness.*

For many of us, we have been way too busy surviving to actually consider what our love might be. We are too tired or stressed to think about such a monumental thing. However, if that's you, then please allow me to kick you a little while you are down. The reason why you are so stressed isn't because you're working so hard but more likely because you are not doing what you love and living on purpose. Love births excitement and releases energy so you operate effortlessly in your personal flow.

> *"Find something you love doing, and you'll retire for the rest of your life."*

Think about a simple example of waking up early in the morning to your alarm clock. How do you feel if your alarm is sounding to let you know it's time to get up and go to a job that you don't love? Do you feel tired? Are you moving quickly or slowly when the feet hit the carpet? What if the very next day when your alarm goes off, it is to let you know it's time to get up because you and your family are leaving on a Hawaiian vacation? Do you feel tired on this day? Are you moving quickly or slowly? The love of family time and memory-building moments from an impending vacation is exciting and energizing! Imagine if you were doing what you truly loved daily? If every job in the world paid the same and you qualified for everything, what would you love to do? Would you be in another profession? The answer is a big clue to your purpose and potentially your Personal Assignment.

The world is full of examples of people who got in touch with their love and developed their God-given gifts. Their contributions are plentiful and will forever be remembered. Wolfgang Amadeus Mozart, the Austrian composer, was 4 years old when he learned his first musical composition. He had a natural gift, a love of music and, thankfully, parents who encouraged his musical development. Imagine if his parents had instead insisted that music was ridiculous and that he should pursue business, medicine or something more mainstream. What would have happened? Mozart lived a brief life of only 35 years yet composed over 600 works and brought joy to generations with his contribution.

According to his mother, Pablo Picasso's first words were, "piz, piz," short for lápiz, meaning pencil in Spanish (ref. Wertenbaker, 9.). He showed a tremendous love and natural gifts towards drawing and by age 7 was receiving formal training by his father. His father was an artist and an instructor who encouraged the young Picasso's passion and felt his son by age 13 had surpassed his ability. The world will forever enjoy, study and collect Picasso's unique work.

But, what about you? You may be thinking that you are not a Mozart or Picasso, and, rest assured, you are right. Instead, you are you with equally impressive gifts waiting to be discovered and pursued. Everyone has passions and gifts. Perhaps you are like most and have not been in touch with them nor pursued them throughout life. You have simply been too busy playing the Simon Says game. If so, now is your time. In fact, lost time is not the reason to feel it is too late but, rather, it should be the reason to feel a sense of urgency! Stop playing Simon Says and get in touch with what you truly love and understand it is directing you toward your Personal Assignment.

CHAPTER 8

Anger is a Clue to Your Personal Assignment

The problem that infuriates you is often the problem you have been designed to solve.
−Mike Murdoch.

I f something crosses your path that truly infuriates you, don't turn your back on it. Don't leave it or avoid it because

> *"Anger is evidence of love."*

of the angry feelings that arise inside you. It has been said that, "Anger is evidence of love." When you are truly angry about something, it is because something you love is being attacked. Most likely you are right on top of your assignment when you consider the things that really infuriate you. Get involved. Take a stand. Do something about it. Use your backbone.

On Thursday, Dec. 1, 1955, Mrs. Rosa Parks finished her work at the Montgomery Fair department store, boarded a city bus, and sat with three other African-Americans in the fifth row — the first row that they were allowed to occupy. A few stops later, the front four rows were filled with whites. One white man was left standing. It was an "established rule" along with Montgomery's segregation law at that time in the

American south that African-American riders not only had to sit in the back rows but were also expected to surrender their seat to a white bus rider if it was needed. Simon said stand and move to the back of the bus. Three complied, but Parks refused. The driver called the police and had Parks arrested.

"People always say that I didn't give up my seat because I was tired, but that isn't true," Parks later explained. "I was not tired physically, or no more tired than I usually was at the end of a working day. . . . No, the only tired I was, was tired of giving in. It was very humiliating having to suffer the indignity of riding segregated buses twice a day, five days a week, to go downtown and work for white people," Parks recalled.

Author Mike Murdoch says, "What you are willing to tolerate, you cannot change." Rosa Parks was not willing to tolerate the mistreatment of African-Americans and, consequently, her life became much more than an isolated incident of defiance of segregation laws but rather it became her lifelong crusade. She is often called "The mother of the civil rights movement."

> "What you are willing to tolerate, you cannot change."
> —Mike Murdoch

The night of Rosa Parks' arrest, word spread quickly due to her reputation as an activist and her network of friends. A meeting was called with African-American community leaders to develop an action plan that included a boycott of the city buses on Monday, when Parks would appear in court. They asked ministers to spread the word at their Sunday sermons and, although some refused, many didn't — including the newly arrived 26-year-old minister, Martin Luther

King, Jr. Within a few days of the boycott, the leaders met, formed an association and elected King as president. In an attempt to determine whether to continue the boycott, they agreed to have a mass meeting that night and put it up to a vote. Seven thousand African-Americans showed up and heard King's words: "There comes a time when people get tired of being trampled over by the iron feet of oppression." They voted unanimously to continue the boycott.

The boycott lasted 381 days, ultimately ending in the Supreme Court where it was ruled that the segregated bus system was unconstitutional. The Montgomery boycott propelled the civil rights movement into national consciousness and Martin Luther King, Jr. became a public figure.

What is it that angers you? What are you not willing to tolerate? Think of the last time you observed something wrong that made you angry. Was somebody mistreated? Was something unjust? Find a problem that infuriates you and you are likely to be on top of your Assignment.

CHAPTER **9**

A Simple Set of Questions

*We learn more by looking for the answer to a question and
not finding it than we do from learning the answer itself.*
–Lloyd Alexander

I was at a quiet border crossing between the United States
and Canada when I was asked a very profound set of questions. I rolled down my car window and the border guard
politely reminded me where I was, "Sir, you are at the United
States / Canada border." This, of course, was comforting information since had I actually been at the United States /
Mexico border I would have really been turned around. Then,
he asked me a set of questions:

"Where are you coming from?"

"Where are you going?"

"How long will you be here?"

"What is the purpose of your trip?"

"Are you bringing anything with you that you intend to
leave behind?"

(He actually asked another question about "carrying fruit"
but that doesn't have any relevance here — unless, perhaps,
your mission has to do with studying the migration methods
of the fruit fly in which case it would be of utmost relevance

to our topic). I thought about his simplistic questions for a moment and wondered how many people have ever been asked such things.

"Where are you coming from?" is a great question. It is important to understand that where we "come from" has given us certain beliefs about the world we live in, and our reality is a direct result of them. Some of our beliefs may be accurate and some may not. The challenge for many people is that an early experience led to an inaccurate belief and their life has been habitually difficult as a direct result. For example, let's suppose that somehow when you were young, an experience led you to believe that $1 + 1 = 9$. You were certain this was true. Unfortunately, since that time, you noticed that anything with finances has been difficult, nothing ever adds up right, and you are convinced that you are just "not smart" when it comes to numbers. The truth is that it has nothing to do with your reasoning, decision-making process or being "smart," but rather you have just been working with a wrong premise. Life would be frustrating, wouldn't it? Hence, the saying, "Don't just work hard, work smart." If the saying, "The secret to success is hard work" was true, wouldn't most people be overflowing with success? Hard work is an ingredient of success but don't try to make the whole cake with it — it isn't going to be very tasty. People work hard. That, typically, isn't the missing link. The key for most is to

> *Personal and spiritual growth takes a long time. In fact, they take a life-time.*

understand that you don't know what you don't know and to begin the process of growth. Personal and spiritual growth takes a long time. In fact, they take a lifetime.

Since there is no way to make quality decisions when you

are operating with inaccurate beliefs, the best investment you can make is in yourself. Make a decision to grow yourself by studying leadership and success principles. Replace bad premises with truths and raise your level of thinking. Be a seeker of God's wisdom. We will discuss this in more detail in Section 3: Pursuing Your Purpose.

As important as my border crossing buddy's first question was, his next questions were enough for me to stop the engine of my car and really begin to think: "Where are you going?" "How long will you be here?" and "What is the purpose of your visit?" I thought to myself, how is it that we must clearly answer those questions to cross a border yet we can travel through life and never consider them at all?

"Where are you going?" There is an old saying, "If you keep doing what you are doing, you are liable to end up exactly where you are headed." The question is whether that is really where you want to go. It is easy to get caught up in the rapid pace of life; hurrying everywhere, jockeying for position, yet never really considering where we are headed. This compulsion to stay in motion more than in thought is fascinating. Why are we heading in the direction that we are? Why are we going there?

"How long will you be here?" Our time on earth is finite, you know? Again, most of us don't ever think about it. Or, if we do, we assume we have much more time than we probably do. What if you knew your departure date? Would it change how you are currently living your life? If so, why not make those changes today?

"What is the purpose of your visit?" The essence of inspiration is understanding your Life Purpose. The significance of your life results from your application of it. What could be more important than clearly understanding why you are visiting?

Finally, his question about what I was going to leave behind literally took my breath away! This guy was like my mentor Dan Williams, challenging me to live a life of significance by leaving a ripple in life that outlasts me. What impact could I make? Wow...this border control guard was deep! The application of your purpose in life is designed to leave a significant impact. May we each pursue and fulfill that mission.

Could you imagine if the only people who were allowed to live in the country were those who could answer these questions with a clear vision of their future? Wow, that would make for some wide-open freeway! In Orrin Woodward and Chris Brady's book, "Launching a Leadership Revolution," they wrote, "The entire Cycle of Achievement begins with vision. Vision is tomorrow's reality expressed as an idea today." The whole idea of having a "dream come true" is obviously based on the concept that one actually has a dream. Imagine that?! It has been said, "Since there is no question that we are all going to die, then the only question is whether we have really lived."

> *"Since there is no question that we are all going to die, then the only question is whether we have really lived."*

I can see it now: "I'm not sure where I'm going, what my purpose is and whether I'm going to leave anything behind, Sir."

"Okay, then pull over to the side. We have no more room for 'wandering generalities' — only 'meaningful specifics'. We have enough boats with broken rudders floating around in here. They are blown this way and that based on the wind with no direction to them at all. What you need to do is chart where you are going in life by developing your Life Purpose Statement. Clearly define your purpose, your Personal Mission, and your assignment as to what you are going to leave behind of significance. Put some purposeful thought into it. Then, come back and see me."

Now, that would be border control, wouldn't it?

CHAPTER 10

Establishing Where You Are

Knowing yourself is the beginning of all wisdom.
—Aristotle

Although it seemed like an obvious statement to me, the border guard began our dialog with clearly establishing where I was at the moment. In hindsight, it makes good sense when traveling to regularly take note of that fact. It is a lot more difficult to get somewhere when you are unclear where you are actually starting from. If you look at a map and find the location of your ultimate destination, what's the next location you look for? You look for your current location so you can then establish the needed journey. We are going to clarify both where you are at and where you are going in order to establish your personal journey. We will start with where you are at currently.

In the book, "The Power to Focus," authors Jack Canfield, Mark Victor Hansen and Les Hewitt propose that you write down in 15-minute intervals throughout the day just what exactly you are doing. Add up the number of activities and notice how many plates you are spinning. Next, notice how much time you are spending on your brilliant areas. Finally, note three things you are doing that you are not good at, don't like or that drains you. Find a plan for others to cover these.

Let's begin with a pop quiz. The good news is I know you will pass. You cannot fail because there is no right or wrong answers. Rather, it is what it is; it is a starting point. So, do your personal best to honestly answer the following questions. Do not put down how you think you should answer. Write down what you truly feel is correct.

LIVING ON-PURPOSE CURRENT ASSESSMENT:

Score each statement between 1 (not at all) and 10 (absolutely true):
___ 1. I have complete clarity of the purpose of my life.
___ 2. My life clearly serves others.
___ 3. My life expresses my life purpose.
___ 4. Those around me clearly know me as my life purpose.
___ 5. I work with those whose values are in alignment with my own.
___ 6. I always consider my values when making decisions.
___ 7. My work brings me great joy.
___ 8. My work fully utilizes my talents and gifts.
___ 9. I am passionate about what I do.
___ 10. I regularly make time for personal restoration.
___ 11. I am not easily discouraged when things don't go as planned.
___ 12. I am doing what I was meant to do.
___ 13. I feel I am fully living my life.
___ 14. I am clear on how I measure my success as a person.
___ 15. I have complete inner peace.
___ **Total** (Note: Your total should fall between 15 and 150).

15 - 40: *Searching*

For those in this category, understand you are not alone. The world is full of people hurting and searching for meaning and purpose in their life. I'm proud of you for stretching yourself. I know that God has a plan for your life which is good. Let this book help you discover it.

41 - 70: *Surviving*

You are working very hard to keep it all going. You have moments of purpose and meaning but, in general, life is more about making it through each day than anything else. You see other people who appear to be happier and more at peace but right now that isn't you. I am proud of you for doing what you can. It is now time for you to feel that peace and live a more on-purpose life.

71 - 100: *Succeeding*

By most people's standards you are succeeding. More than not you feel good about your life and your life reflects it. You have general clarity and a sense of direction and meaning. However, inside you know that there is a lot more fulfillment that you wish to obtain.

101 - 130: *Significance is clearly defining your life!*

Congratulations, you are living a life oriented around significance. You have great clarity of purpose and feel tremendous peace and fulfillment. Your life has meaning and is making a difference in the lives of others. You are an inspiration.

131 - 150: *Inspired On-purpose Life*

You are a rare individual. Your life is a masterpiece with clarity of purpose and meaning. You feel truly at peace and are a significant blessing to others in the world. You are living an inspired life!

A BALANCED LIFE?

The next part of determining where you are in life is to assess the balance you are living. We are all excelling in some areas and falling short in others. Often, however, it is difficult to take a clear snapshot of yourself. The "wheel of life," as it's often referred to, is a great way to take a clear, objective look at the balance you have in your life. If you have ever attempted to ride a bicycle with a wheel that isn't true, you quickly feel uncomfortable. The greater the imbalance of the wheel, the greater the discomfort you experience. With a certain degree of imbalance, the bicycle is no longer rideable. The objective of this exercise is to establish a clear, graphic picture of your life wheel. If you were to attempt to ride a bicycle with the wheels of your life, how would it feel? Again, answer honestly. The goal here is to get an accurate picture that can act as a starting point.

Life is composed of eight different domains. They are the following:

1. Spiritual — relationship with God, prayer, worship, fellowship, faith, spiritual practices
2. Family — immediate, extended, social family of friends, romance
3. Work — vocation, career, volunteer work, service
4. Leisure — fun, play, travel
5. Physical — health, fitness
6. Financial — earning, tithing, saving, donating, spending money
7. Educational — reading, audio learning programs, seminars, classes, study groups, personal growth
8. Creative — writing, cooking, gardening, painting, crafting

Each area represents a domain or a slice of the pie representing your life. The objective is to live with balance in your life by excelling in not just one area but in all of them. The reason this is important is because each domain is connected with the others. That is, there is a direct correlation between how well you are doing in one domain with each of the other ones. Often, it is most obvious to see the least effective domain negatively affecting the others. For example, perhaps you are not doing well in the physical domain. Do you believe if your physical body was having problems that it would affect your work, your family, etc.? If you lacked leisure time, do you suppose it would affect your family, your physical heath, etc.? Make it more extreme and it really becomes obvious. Let's say the physical life was really bad...as in you died. How would that affect the other domains? What if the financial domain just declared bankruptcy — how would that make an impact? Would a divorce in the family domain cause an affect with the others? By understanding the connectivity between all eight domains, we can see the importance of not letting one domain fall seriously short, as it will inevitably negatively affect each of the others.

Another more positive way of looking at it is by increasing our performance level within a domain it will have a positive impact on each of the others. This, of course, is assuming you didn't sacrifice the performance of another to achieve it. For example, as your physical domain improves with better diet or exercise it will have a positive effect on your work (more energy), on your family (feel better about yourself, may motivate others), etc. However, if you sacrificed valuable family time to do it, causing a negative impact on the family domain, the net difference will be the overall result. The areas of restoration (leisure, creative, spiritual, etc) balance the work domain. Without "rest-oration," you will not be able to work at full effectiveness. Every domain affects the others positively or negatively.

CREATE A LIFE WHEEL

Step 1: For each domain, rate your level of satisfaction on a scale of 0 - 10. A zero is the extreme worst case scenario. A ten is as good as it could be.

Satisfaction Level   **Domain**

(0 -10)

_____ Spiritual — relationship with God, prayer, worship, fellowship, faith, spiritual practices

_____ Family — immediate, extended, social family of friends, romance

_____ Work — vocation, career, volunteer work, service

_____ Leisure — fun, play, travel

_____ Physical — health, fitness

_____ Financial — earning, tithing, saving, donating, spending money

_____ Educational — reading, audio learning programs, seminars, classes, study groups, personal growth

_____ Creative — writing, cooking, gardening, painting, crafting

Step 2: Plot your answers on the Wheel of Life below as shown in the example (note: zero is the center and ten is the outside):

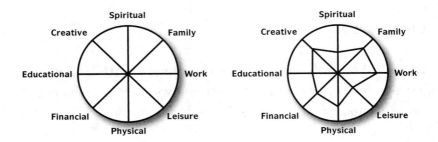

Step 3: Connect your plot points and shade in the area from the center out. The shaded area is your personal Life Wheel. How does it look? This is the wheel you have been riding around on. Could it be more in balance? The good news is that all this represents is where you currently are at in your life. It is a snapshot. It is the current results of your past decisions. It is your starting point, and certainly not necessarily your ending point. Now, let's take a look at where we are going.

CHAPTER 11

Creating Your Life Purpose Statement

A successful life is one that is lived through understanding and pursuing one's own path, not chasing after the dreams of others.
—Chin-Ning Chu

Your Life Purpose Statement is the ultimate clarity of your life. It sets a valuable course for you. It guides you through making difficult decisions. It makes it apparent when you are off the course of your purposeful direction and leads you back to the proper heading. Although parts of it will develop over time, your Life Purpose Statement describes who you are and what you stand for. It defines what is most important in life and what success looks like to you. It also describes your God-given purpose as well as the service to others that your purpose can uniquely fulfill. Specifically, it is the combination of your Personal Mission Statement, your Purpose, and your Personal Assignment in life. Many people have heard of the concept or relate it as something similar to a company vision or mission statement. However, most have never completed a Life Purpose Statement. It can seem overwhelming and confusing. It can be difficult to even determine where to start.

The following process will keep it all very simple. The answers are already inside of you. The key to discovering those answers is in asking the right questions. Answer the questions below and discover the real you. Understand that there are no right answers. Really try to answer the questions honestly and don't fall into answering them the way you feel you *should* answer them. It's easy to respond with a popular Simon Says answer, but seriously search your heart for your personal truth. Your answers aren't supposed to be like everyone else's — your uniqueness is what makes you special.

It is also really important that you create the right environment for this exercise. Before you even start, set yourself up in a quiet, relaxing location. Take a little time to relax from the stresses of your world. Take some deep breaths and let your mind go. You will be taking a look inside yourself during this process and the more relaxed you are, the better it will flow. Realize that you don't need to complete it all in one sitting. Take any pressure off of yourself. You can always take a break and come back to it.

Finally, for some, this may be a scary exercise. Many people have buried some of this stuff very well. Ironically, often the things that we are meant to do we bury so we don't need to face them. I want those who struggle with this emotionally to know that you are not alone. There are many people who feel the exact same way as you do. Let your life experience the fulfillment it is supposed to enjoy, by allowing it the opportunity to clearly connect with what it is truly designed to do. Just remember the short-term fear to overcome, although potentially tough, will be far less challenging than swallowing the regret you will have as you end your life knowing you never did what you were meant to do.

I applaud you in advance for investing the time and effort of actually completing this process of defining your Life Purpose. It's not just an exercise, a puzzle, or some "interesting thoughts" to read about. It's your life! What could be more important to actually clarify? The scary thing is that if you do not define your Life Purpose, I assure you that someone else will do it for you. Unfortunately, if you allow others to define it for you, it will most certainly be the Life Purpose that is best for them. So, congratulations in advance.

> *The scary thing is that if you do not define your Life Purpose, I assure you that someone else will do it for you.*

We will take each item — Personal Mission Statement, your Purpose, and your Personal Assignment — work through them step-by-step and in the end you will have developed a Life Purpose Statement. Certainly, there are many methods available to make this happen. However, the following process is simple, fun and effective. You will be amazed what will happen through this process. Enjoy.

YOUR PERSONAL MISSION STATEMENT

The development process of your Personal Mission Statement will include discovering your core values, prioritizing them, and defining the vision of what success with each of them looks like. Putting the vision of these successfully fulfilled core values together gives you a personal mission or target to achieve. Your core values define who you are and what you stand for in life. They are the things that mean the most to you — the things for which you would give your life.

They do not change over time; they are the constant core of who you are.

By uncovering and discovering your core values you are immediately given a guide for life. Since they are the most valuable thing in life to you, they should govern your actions on your quest for success. What would be the point in achieving success in something only to sacrifice something you value more (one of your core values)? Decision making is much simpler as everything you do can be checked with your core values to see that it is in alignment. For example, it may be easier in the moment of something to simply tell a lie. However, the more you value honesty, the more you will be guided toward the decision to tell the truth. Making decisions that maintain alignment between your actions and your core values is a key to inner peace. In other words, often people are having internal conflict and even diminished self-esteem because either consciously or unconsciously they are doing something that isn't in alignment with their core values. They aren't "supporting themselves."

> *Making decisions that maintain alignment between your actions and your core values is a key to inner peace.*

By prioritizing your core values, you will have the ability to make the best decision possible even when it seems to trigger conflicting core values. For example, let's say one of your core values is Family and another is Financial Security. You are offered a promotion which would greatly increase your financial security. However, the promotion requires moving to another part of the country or dedicating more time to work which *you believe* would not be good for the family. While the promotion appears to support one Core Value (Financial

Security), it also appears to be in conflict with another (Family). What do you do? With prioritized core values, you can see which you value more and it should guide your decision. The only time to compromise a value is for a higher value. If you compromised your values for any other reason other than a higher value (eg., because it was easier), you would lose self-respect and, consequently, self-esteem.

Another example of the importance of prioritizing your core values can be seen in the business world: Imagine a board of a non-profit alcohol-recovery center learns of a large donation being offered by a beer company. Should the board accept the donation? Some members would say, "Absolutely. We need the money and it can help a lot of people." Meanwhile, other members would say, "Not a chance. This company sells what we are helping people recover from the abuse of [alcohol]. It would be hypocrisy." Without having pre-established, prioritized core values, there is no clear guide and, most likely, it will be one conflicted board meeting.

If you haven't noticed, your mind is often like a boardroom with many thoughts running back and forth. The key to peace is to be grounded with prioritized core values that are ready to take the lead at any moment of your life where there are important decisions to be made. What is interesting is that without this process, not only will we trade our peace for anxiety but rather than core value-based decision making we tend to default to fear-based decision making. That is, since we don't have clarity, we fall back to a protective, survival instinct. We tend to do what we feel is safest. This perspective will be based on the beliefs that we have formed from our experiences in life. Referring back to the earlier example, if you had an experience that gave you an inner fear of family loss, most likely you will do what is best for family. However, if you had an experience that gave you an inner fear of financial insecurity, most likely you will do what is best financially. Now, your decision process is based on past trauma and the avoidance of the manifestation of your fears. What if you have developed a fear of financial loss but truly valued family well above financial security? Without prioritizing your core values, your fear will lead you to choose what is best financially; exactly opposite of your core value priorities. Hence, whether fear-based decision making results in supporting what you truly value or not is now a matter of chance. You are trying to move forward successfully in your life but are governed by fears developed from your past. Odds are over time, this process won't lead to your ultimate fulfillment.

Finally, by defining what success looks like with your core values, you have clarified a vision of your future. You now have a target to strive towards. You are not just wandering through life but have a specific destination. In addition, it offers an ability to fulfill our innate desire to score our life. We love to score things. Nearly everything in this world is scored or ranked, but how do you do it with a life? Many score it by accumulation of wealth. It is an easy scorecard as the highest number wins; $5,000,000 beats $1,000,000, four cars and a boat beat one car and a surfboard. "He or she with the most toys wins!" Right? Well, it is one way to score life but, as most come to learn, it isn't a good representation of your fulfillment in life. Wealth can be a wonderful blessing and I enjoy nice things as much as anyone. However, when your life comes to its end here on earth, the stuff stays. What will matter is who you became during your journey. What came of the things you valued most (i.e., your core values)? Are you full of regrets or did you achieve your vision? If you must score your life, score it by the successful fulfillment of God's Purpose for your life including your vision for your core values.

Step 1: Discovering what You Value

Suppose I had a tightrope that I placed on my floor from one end of the room to the other. If I offered you $100 to walk on it across the room, I'm sure you would do it. Why not? It's like free money. No risk or real effort and a $100 reward. Great. Now, suppose I hung that tightrope between the Petronas Towers in Malaysia. They stand approximately 1,400 feet tall and, until 2004, were classified as the world's tallest buildings. There you are a quarter mile high on top one of the towers while I am at the top of the other encouraging you to walk across that same rope as before. I offer you the same $100. Do you do it? What about for $1,000? $1,000,000? Obviously, it's not free money anymore. The risk is death and it wouldn't be worth it unless your name is Blondin (aka Jean François Gravelet) who crossed the gorge below Niagara Falls on a tightrope so many times that at one point he stopped midway, sat, cooked and ate an omelet.

However, suppose I'm not encouraging you and offering you a cash reward to walk across but rather I have your child (or some very meaningful person in your life) and I'm threatening to drop him/her if you don't immediately come. What is your response now? You don't even think about it, do you? The person I am holding is so priceless that you would do whatever it takes to save them.

The question is, "What other things will create that kind of emotion within you?" What things do you value so much that you would cross the rope to save me from dropping them out of your life? Rate the items below according to their value to you and write it in at the bottom any important values that are not included.

1 = You would let me drop it — you definitely would not cross to save it.
2 = You probably would let me drop it — you likely would not cross to save it.
3 = You aren't sure — maybe, maybe not.
4 = You probably would not let me drop it — you likely would cross to save it.
5 = You would not let me drop it — you definitely would cross to save it.

		Used in Section 3: Pursuing your Life Purpose	
Value Rating (1-5)		**Behavior**	**Action Step**
Honesty	1 2 3 4 5		
Courage	1 2 3 4 5		
Fairness	1 2 3 4 5		
Peace	1 2 3 4 5		
Integrity	1 2 3 4 5		
Power	1 2 3 4 5		
Wealth	1 2 3 4 5		
Joy	1 2 3 4 5		
Acceptance	1 2 3 4 5		
Influence	1 2 3 4 5		
Happiness	1 2 3 4 5		
Love	1 2 3 4 5		

Justice   1 2 3 4 5
Success   1 2 3 4 5
Recognition   1 2 3 4 5
Faith   1 2 3 4 5
Friendship   1 2 3 4 5
Family   1 2 3 4 5
Career   1 2 3 4 5
Fame   1 2 3 4 5
Truth   1 2 3 4 5
Status   1 2 3 4 5
Personal
  Appearance 1 2 3 4 5
Personal
  Growth   1 2 3 4 5
Spiritual
  Growth   1 2 3 4 5
Authenticity 1 2 3 4 5
Wisdom   1 2 3 4 5
Excellence   1 2 3 4 5
Health   1 2 3 4 5
Legacy   1 2 3 4 5
Security   1 2 3 4 5
Tradition   1 2 3 4 5
_____   1 2 3 4 5
_____   1 2 3 4 5
_____   1 2 3 4 5
_____   1 2 3 4 5

Next, go back through the items and circle the six with the highest score. If there is a tie with more than six, pick the top six that really resonate with you.

Now, with only six remaining, picture us back atop the towers. I am going to drop three of them. I will automatically drop the three with the lowest scores. However, if there is a tie, which three do you tell me to let go? Only three may remain. Cross the others off.

Finally, rank the top three in order of priority by writing a #1, #2, and #3 next to them accordingly. If there is a tie, which would you tell me to let go first? Mark it #3. What do you tell me to let go of next? Mark it #2. What remains is the one thing that you will get to keep forever. Mark it #1.

Congratulations, you have just listed the three things you value most in your life.

Step 2: Defining Success with Your Core Values

Rewrite your top three core values in order to complete the sentence below, "The three things I value most are..." Then, for each item, simply complete a statement of how it is that you would know you are successful with it? Picture being at the end of your life and saying "Success in my life means..." For example, if you put "excellence", how is it that you are successful in your life with regards to excellence? You may write: *"Excellence*: Success in my life means... that I always do my best. More important than how well I do is the knowledge that I have given it my all. I strive to regularly learn and grow to improve my performances and regardless of how large or small, how mundane or exciting, how difficult or easy the task may be, I always give it my personal best."

Now, fill in your three definitions.

The three things I value most are: _____,
_____, and _____.

1. _____: Success in my life means..._____
_____
_____

2. _____: Success in my life means... _____
_____
_____

3. _____: Success in my life means... _____
_____
_____

Congratulations, you have just defined success with your top three core values! This process, although simple, clearly defined your core values and what needs to happen to achieve success with them. Fulfilling the vision of success with these core values as you described becomes your personal mission.

Step 3: Creating Your Personal Mission Statement

Merge your three core value vision statements into one on the lines below by starting with, "Success in my life means" and following it with your three answers.

_____
_____
_____
_____
_____

Congratulations! You have just created your Personal Mission Statement for your life!

YOUR PURPOSE STATEMENT

Your purpose is who God designed you to be. It is not about *doing*, but rather it's about *being*. Your purpose is a matter of becoming who you were meant to be. I know this may twist the mind slightly, but it is important to understand. Hang with me. Too often people struggle to discover their purpose because they start within the wrong context. They ask, "What am I supposed to be doing?" It's the wrong question. What you do is simply an *expression* of who you ARE. In other words, the application of your purpose is seen in what you do. Remember, we are human-beings, not human doings. When you clarify your purpose as to who you are meant to be, it can apply to every area of your life. That is, when you have discovered your purpose, it will not only apply to your vocation, but also to your personal life, your spiritual life, etc. Consequently, you will be *doing* different things — things that all are extending from your purpose of being. For example, my purpose is to be a leader, a teacher and an inspiration. I will apply that to my family in one way and I will apply that in my vocation in another way.

> *When you clarify your purpose as to who you are meant to be, it can apply to every area of your life.*

If your purpose doesn't apply to one area of your life, then you confused an expression of your purpose (e.g., your vocation) with your actual purpose. For example, an individual mentioned that he or she felt their purpose was to be a graphic designer. However, graphic design work isn't applicable to all areas of life so it couldn't be his purpose. Searching further he realized that his purpose is more clearly defined in being creative. This he is able to apply with his family, his church, and in every area of his life. Graphic design work was simply one way he was able to express his creativity. He simply spent so much time at work that it dominated the thought of his purpose.

Why is this distinction so important — between being and doing? It is important because if you wrap your purpose around doing, what happens when you can no longer do it? Too often we all hear stories about the guy who dies 18 months after he retires. What's up with that? Well, it's been said that a person can live 30 days without food, three days without water, three minutes without air, but not even three seconds without hope. When a person wraps their purpose around their work and they retire, they suddenly have lost their purpose! Without a purpose, there is no hope for fulfillment in life. Similarly, if a person wraps their purpose around their role, such as being a mom, what happens when the kids leave home? Not only would that mother need to process the natural emotions of their child leaving, but they would also need to process the departure of their purpose. As subtle as this distinction may currently seem, it won't seem subtle at all when such an event actually occurs in your life. Define your purpose around *being* and then apply it to work, family and every area of your life. Changes in your life will occur, but your purpose will always stay secure and constant.

Step 1: Clarifying Your Desires

Your purpose is linked to your desires and gifts. This should make sense; you are interested in and good at some things for a reason. The irony is that many people miss their purpose because it does come naturally and they discount it or overlook it, searching for something more difficult. Since life is typically so challenging, we have been trained to endure discomfort and begin to expect it. Don't discount your gifts! Just because they come naturally to you and you enjoy them isn't reason to think it isn't what you are designed to be about. The fact is, they probably have a lot to do with who you are designed to be! What many of us are unaware of is what you think is so simple, others can't imagine. And, if you tried to teach someone else your gift, you would probably struggle a lot. Why? Because it is often difficult to explain what comes naturally. The best teachers are those teaching areas that they really had to learn themselves.

Often what you love to do can also be what you are naturally good at doing. Begin by writing down all the things you love doing such as teaching, writing, inspiring, serving, etc. Use words that end with "ing." Be sure to write down what *you* really think and not what you believe you are *supposed to think*. The following is a list of some possibilities; it certainly is not complete list but serves as a start and to trigger other thoughts within you.

teaching	writing	leading	speaking
analyzing	mentoring	coaching	reading
persuading	exploring	supporting	healing
solving	inspiring	researching	managing
comforting	entertaining	caring	negotiating
traveling	repairing	uplifting	encouraging
developing	growing	inventing	organizing
building	clarifying		

'ing Favorites:

_____

_____

_____

_____

_____

_____

_____

_____

_____

_____

_____

_____

_____

_____

Next, read through your list and circle your top three. Then, read the circled items and notice how each of them makes you feel. Do one or two stand out more than the other(s)? If so, eliminate it down to that one or two.

Step 2: Clarifying Your Gifts

The next step is go beyond your interests and look at your gifts. Dick Richards, author of "Are You Using Your Genius at Work?" writes, "Your Purpose is a specific external expression of your genius. It is one of your gifts and it lies behind your experience and talents." His book is an excellent reference for clarifying your Genius. For some people the concept of looking at their gifts, let alone their "Genius," is a very difficult one. This is either because we struggle with believing we really have gifts and value to others or because we have been ingrained not to think so richly of ourselves. However, we all have gifts and are able to give others something of value. Dig deep and think about it as you answer each of the following questions.

Desire: Often what we naturally desire to do is something that we are actually gifted at doing. Yes, there are exceptions but often it is the case. Looking at your top picks of the things you love to do most in Step 1, answer the following "desire" question: "Which of my desires do I believe I am naturally gifted at doing?" __

_____

_____

_____.

Value: We often use our gifts regularly without typically even being aware of it. Others will pick up on them and gravitate to us for our assistance. Thinking about what others seek from us or simply what we provide others is a clue to our gifts. Answer the "value" question: "When people come to you, what are they usually looking to receive from you?" That is, "What value do you seem to be able to provide others?"

_____

_____

_____.

Success: Think of times when you experienced success

— large or small. During each of those times, there was something that you contributed to help bring that success about. Answer the "success" question: "When you have experienced success, what did you contribute to help bring it about?" _____

_____

_____

_____.

Step 3: Discovering Your Purpose

Let your purpose revel itself. Look at your answers in Step 2 and, using that information, write the answer to the following:

My Purpose is to be: _____

_____.

Now, read your Purpose Statement out loud. How does it resonate with you internally? What do you feel? Did you hit the mark? Discovering your purpose is less analytical and more intuitive. More than thinking to figure it out, you feel it. You experience it. You will know when it's right. Either you'll feel — "Yes, that's it...that's right!" — or it'll be more like, "No, that's not quite it yet." If it isn't quite right, then rewrite it again until you feel you have hit it. Take the time to re-write it as many times as necessary until you really feel it. An extremely short example may look like:

"My Purpose is to be a teacher." — the teacher feels right on but there's a little more.

"My Purpose is to be an encourager and an inspiration." —

feels good but the teacher part is key.

"My Purpose is to be an encourager and a teacher." — that's it! That is right on! That is the combination for me!

Finally, referring back to your Life Segments chart from earlier, verify that the Purpose Statement you wrote can be applied to all areas of your life. If it doesn't, then ask, "How can I simplify my answer so that it can be applied to all areas of my life but still maintain the root of what I'm 'bringing to the table?'" Most likely you just applied your purpose to one area of your life. If it does apply to all areas of your life, congratulations! You have done what very few people have ever done…you have looked within and discovered your purpose given and reveled from above.

Your Personal Assignment

Everyone has been given a specific purpose with unique gifts and talents. Your purpose is intended to be applied to all areas of your life so that you can serve others most effectively and experience life to its fullest. It is also designed to solve a specific problem. That is, there is some specific problem that you are uniquely designed to solve. It is that something that gets you passionate and for which your uniqueness can have an impact. As we discussed earlier, your emotions are a huge clue as to what this is specifically for you. Something grabs you emotionally. It makes you angry, desperately sad, or some combination of these or other strong emotions and it is calling you to do something about it. Your Personal Assignment is the application of your purpose to this calling.

In Viktor Frankl's world-renowned book, "Man's Search for Meaning," he wrote

"One should not search for an abstract meaning of life. Everyone has his own specific vocation or mission in life to carry out a concrete assignment, which demands fulfillment. Therein he cannot be replaced, nor can his life be repeated. Thus, everyone's task is as unique as is his specific opportunity to implement it."

Step 1: Identifying the Problem

Considering the things that stir you up the most inside — as just said, the things that make you angry, desperately sad, or some combination of these or other strong emotions — answer the following question: "If you could change one thing, what would it be? It must be the thing that emotionally grabs you. It may be a world issue, a national issue, or a community issue. What one thing would it be?" _____

_____

_____.

Step 2: Clarifying Your Vision

A vision is the way you picture how something can be. It has two parts: Who and What. "Who" is those to which your vision includes. "What" is the picture you see resulting. Now, take your answer from the question above and complete the following Vision Statement: My vision is for *(who does it include)* to *(describe the change as you picture it to be)*. For example, let's say your answer above was the one thing you would change in the world is to eliminate starvation among all children. Consequently, your vision statement could read: My vision is for *all children of the world* to *be fed*.

Write your Vision Statement: My vision is for _____ _____to _____ _____.

Read your Vision Statement out loud. How does it resonate with you internally? What do you feel? Does it trigger passion inside of you? Does it bring tears to your eyes when you really think about it? If not, go back to the question and keep digging till you get in touch with something that truly matters to you. If it does trigger that passion within you, then congratulations! You have just defined your ultimate vision.

Step 3: Establishing Your Personal Assignment

Your Personal Assignment is the application of your purpose to your calling in order to fulfill your ultimate vision. A vision develops over time and so does its corresponding plan. Although a complete answer may not come to you all at once, answer the following question regarding your above vision: "How can I use my purpose to contribute to the fulfillment of my vision?" _____

_____

_____

_____

_____

_____

_____

Regularly ask yourself the question above, "How can I use my purpose to contribute to the fulfillment of my vision?" By doing so, greater clarity and insights will continue to emerge. Congratulations! You have just clarified your Personal Assignment.

You have now completed all the components of your Life Purpose Statement. The final step is to combine them into one statement. Start with your Mission Statement, and then add your Purpose and Personal Assignment statements. You may wish to use the following outline:

Life Purpose Statement

My Personal Mission is to live a life yielding _____
_____
_____
_____
_____.

My God-given Purpose is to _____
_____
_____.

My Personal Assignment is to _____
_____
_____
_____
_____

I commit my life, including all my energy, focus, and resources towards the fulfillment of my Life Purpose.

Congratulations! You have completed your Life Purpose Statement! You are a meaningful specific; no longer a wondering generality. Post your Life Purpose Statement proudly. Read it daily. See it happening. Feel it inside. And, keep it updated. It is important to remember that your Purpose and core values are constant. They don't change—they are uniquely you. However, the application of your purpose and core values will change as your visions and corresponding missions develop over time. As you experience more of life, you will discover new passions. This is why it is so important to stay in touch with your feelings as you realize new tragedies or miracles of your own and of others. Those that generate passion within may be revealing a new vision or calling that shouldn't be ignored. Explore it. And, as needed, update your Life Purpose Statement.

Section 3

Pursuing Your
Life Purpose
THE TOOLS TO EMPOWER YOUR PURSUIT

CHAPTER 12

Dream - Struggle - Victory

Believe me, the reward is not so great without the struggle.
—Wilma Rudolph

Let the journey begin! In the pursuit of the fulfillment of your Life Purpose, you will experience tremendous energy, joy and peace. There is nothing that

> *Is what you are doing with your life fulfilling your Life Purpose?*

you can buy or win that will ever compare to the satisfaction of knowing that you are living in alignment with your Life Purpose or simply living an "on-purpose" life. Yes, you will have ups and downs but, understand, that is all part of your journey. You will have victories and you will also have challenges. The challenges will enable you to achieve more victories. It's all a part of the process. But, I'm getting ahead of myself. Let's look at this journey one step at a time.

First, let's revisit where you are at in your life. You have already identified the balance in your life through the Wheel of Life process. Next, consider the following serious question.

It is one of the most important questions that you could ever ask. Ready? Here it is: Is what you are doing with your life fulfilling your Life Purpose? Is it, really? At the end of your life, are you going to be able to look back with deep satisfaction knowing that you achieved great success with the things you value most? If your answer is no, then *WHY* are you doing it? Why would you be doing what is not fulfilling your Life Purpose? Before you answer, don't say, "Because of the money." I know money is important. Believe me, I understand. I have had money and not had money and I prefer to have it. Money is necessary; it's a great tool, and you can do wonderful things with it. However, it's not about the money.

Don't fall into the "I'm stuck" trap. You're not stuck. You may be wedged in a little, but you're not stuck.

Money should never direct your life. Don't let it get a grip on you. Don't let it define you. Remember, nobody really wants money — after all, it is just paper with pictures of past leaders on it, right? All that people want is what money can provide. However, if you really dig deeper to determine what money is really touching emotionally, I would submit to you that many of those emotions (happiness, respect, peace, security, etc.) will be connected with more richly through personal growth and the pursuit of your Life Purpose than through a financial purchase. As author Steve Pavlina has written, "If you think money will buy you security, then go to work directly on your fears and

> *"If you think money will buy you security, then go to work directly on your fears and insecurities and develop your capacity for courage. If you think money will buy you a sense of abundance, then focus on overcoming your lack of appreciation for what you already have, and begin to live with an attitude of gratitude."*
> —*Steve Pavlina*

insecurities and develop your capacity for courage. If you think money will buy you a sense of abundance, then focus on overcoming your lack of appreciation for what you already have, and begin to live with an attitude of gratitude."

Consider what your life would be like if you followed your passion first over the pursuit of money. Again, I am not suggesting that making money is bad; make a lot of it and use it for good — that is wonderful and needed —nor am I suggesting to be irresponsible or irrational. However, I am suggesting that placing the pursuit of your Life Purpose ahead of the pursuit of making money will lead to far more enriched life. It is also possible that you may find a way to create an income source from your passion. In such a situation, the more you did what you loved, the more income you would make and the more you could continue to do it. Now what you love and making money are no longer in conflict with one another. That is, you are no longer doing one thing to make money and squeezing in another because you love it. Rather, your life reflects your love.

Looking at it another way, what if you only had 18 months to live? Would you change anything about your life? If so, what would it be and why would you wait?! What if you never get your "warning?"

A doctor tells a patient, "I have good news and bad news — which do you want first?"

"The good news," the patient replies.

"Okay. You only have 24 hours to live," says the doctor.

"Oh my!" The patient replies. "If that is the good news than what is the bad news?"

"The bad news is I forgot to tell you yesterday."

A silly joke, yes, but a profound point: Your time may be

up at any moment. Consequently, why wait? Live for what really matters NOW!

Whatever you do, don't tell me it's too late for you. It's never too late. If your heart is beating and your mind is thinking, then you are here for a reason. You have a mission to fulfill and the clock is ticking so let's get rolling. You are one decision away from changing your life. Given

> *If your heart is beating and your mind is thinking, then you are here for a reason.*

the entire purpose you are on this planet in the first place is to fulfill your Life Purpose, doesn't it seem a bit ridiculous to make excuses as to why you can't do it? Of course you can do it. It's a matter of making some adjustments. Now, this isn't a suggestion to drop all of your responsibilities, dress in camouflage, and run off into the hills because you feel you are being called to study nature. Perhaps you'll get there — it's your mission — but, for now, I'm suggesting that you take a good look at your life and say to yourself, "If I keep doing what I am doing, I'm liable to end up where I'm headed. Consequently, do I believe that activity will fulfill my Life Purpose? Is that what I'm all about?" And, if not, make a decision to start redesigning your life responsibly so it will. Do it now! After all, life isn't a dress rehearsal; this is it! This is your one spectacular performance. Helen Keller said it best: "Life is a daring, bold adventure or nothing at all."

Here is the outline for your journey: Dream - Struggle - Victory. The process is the same for any worthwhile endeavor. You start with a dream — a picture of what the achievement will look like. Next, you encounter and grow through a set of struggles. Finally, you achieve the victory for which you have fought. Now, if we had the opportunity to vote on this process, most of us would like to adjust it to: Dream - Victory. Let's eliminate the "Struggle" part. Sure, that sounds lots more fun. Dream it and enjoy the victory. Simple. Ironically, however, your greatest reward will in fact be what you become as a result of your struggles in route to your victory. That is, your true victory is the developed you from the struggle, more than the victory itself. It's not what you achieve that truly counts but who you become in the process. Consequently, let me say I hope you struggle a lot — it will make a better you! Thomas Paine said, "I love the man that can smile in trouble, that can gather strength from distress, and grow brave by reflection. 'Tis the business of little minds to shrink but he whose heart is firm, and whose conscience approves his conduct, will pursue his principles unto death."

Fortunately, the process doesn't start with the struggle; it starts with the dream. Your dream is necessary to motivate you through the struggles. Without a dream first, nothing happens. It was Aug. 28, 1963 on the steps of the Lincoln Memorial, when one of the defining moments in the American civil rights movement occurred in front of over 200,000 people as Martin Luther King, Jr. passionately shared the words, "I have a Plan..." Or, was it, "I have a Dream..." The plan wouldn't have inspired the people to pay the price of the following struggle, but the casting of a dream did. I hope you build the dream of your life to be big. I hope it gives you goosebumps! I hope it is big enough that you realize you can't do it by yourself and, consequently, find yourself humbly falling to your knees for help. Doesn't it make sense to ask God for help? What could you accomplish with Him as your partner?

So, where do you start? Ralph Waldo Emerson said, "The

ancestor of every action is a thought." The journey of a thousand miles may begin with a single step but the thought of that step came first. If the thought failed to yield any belief that it was possible even to take a single step then the journey would have ended before it even started. The point is this journey all begins in our head. Robert Schuller has a famous question: "What would you do if you knew you couldn't fail?" It's a great question because it forces us to think about what we would go after if we were guaranteed success — it tells us what is meaningful to us. Let's face it, nobody likes the idea of failing and only a few actually like change (I

> *The pain of change is temporary and much less than the deep pain of regret.*

know, babies and customers do). But, the pain of change is temporary and much less than the deep pain of regret. Do you really want to get to the end of your life and be full of regrets? Of course not. Nobody sits around saying, "You know, I'm not going to do this because then I can look back late in life with deep, sorrowful regret." No, typically the thought is much more simple: "I don't want to," "I don't feel like it," or "I'm afraid." The problem is what you really don't want or wish you didn't feel is regret later in life. Mark Twain said, "Twenty years from now you will be more disappointed by the things that you didn't do than by the ones you did do. So throw off the bowlines. Sail away from the safe harbor. Catch the trade winds in your sails. Explore. Dream. Discover." Courage, of course, is your key. Have the courage to move forward with your life. "Whatever you do, you need courage. Whatever course you decide upon, there is always someone to tell you that you are wrong. There are always difficulties arising that tempt you to believe your critics are right. To map out a course of action and follow it to an end requires some of the same courage that a soldier needs. Peace has its victories, but it takes brave men and women to win them" — Ralph Waldo Emerson.

I was running in a half-marathon race in Laguna Hills, CA over a Memorial Day weekend. Just prior to the event, I asked my son Chase, who was 3, if he would like to run in the kids' race the day before. The day before the half-marathon, there were several kids' races including a 25-yard diaper dash for the youngest kids. He enthusiastically agreed and we signed him (and his just-turned 2-year-old brother, Casey) up for the race. He was excited! Playing it up, I took them to the store and we purchased matching running outfits with shoes that lit up each time they took a step — more lights, more fun, you know? We even practiced, "Ready, set, go!" with sprints across the family room. The day of the race arrived and we trotted down to the event site. We checked in, pinned their race bib numbers to their shirts and they were ready to go. Noticing that the older kids were already running the half-mile and one-mile races, we went alongside the course, stood and cheered. I was holding my youngest boy Casey and Chase was standing beside me. Moments later I realized that I was the only one still cheering. Chase had stopped clapping and was quiet. Next, I felt a little tap on my leg. I looked down and there was his outstretched arm reaching up towards me with his race bib torn off his shirt and crumpled up in his hand.

"What's the matter?" I asked with concern.

"I don't want to run anymore," Chase responded.

"Why?" I asked.

"I just don't want to," he said with a solemn look his face. I took his number and picked him up. I began to walk, talking to my two boys that I was now carrying.

"Have you ever heard of the word 'courage'?" I asked them. Chase shook his head no. "Courage is when you do something because it's the right thing to do even though you are scared," I told him. "Did you know that Daddy gets scared sometimes?" I asked.

They were both looking and listening but neither responded. "Sometimes Daddy speaks in front of thousands of people and it can be scary. Sometimes Daddy is about to begin one of his ultra-running 100+ mile races and he knows it will hurt a lot and that can be scary. But, I do it anyway and afterward I'm always so glad that I did." I walked around for a few minutes, all three of us quiet now.

Then, very softly, Chase said, "Daddy, I'm scared too."

"What are you scared about?" I asked. He looked at me silently as tears began to well up in his eyes. "Hey Chase," I asked. "Since this is your first race, what do you think about us doing it together? Do you think we could do it if we did it together?"

"I think so," he responded with the slightest of smiles.

"Okay. Let's all three run it together." We walked over to the start line and I put Chase down; I was still holding Casey. It was a whole lot of 2- and 3-year-olds, and Daddy. I definitely had the size advantage in this one. The race starter announced, "Ready, set...," and then "bang!" The gun went off and immediately I felt a huge squeeze on my hand. It was Chase. He was looking up at me with intensity and then together we all took our first step. We walked the whole way and Chase never took his eyes off of me. After we finished, a volunteer ran over and put finishing medals around my boys' necks. Chase grabbed the medal and said with sheer excitement, "Look Daddy, my first medal! I'm going to put it up on the wall like the ones you have!" I asked him, "How do you feel?" He said, "Great! I was scared but I did it!" A couple of weeks later after nap time, Chase came downstairs with his running outfit on. "Hey buddy, what are you wearing?" I asked. "I'm wearing my favorite outfit," he said. "I just put it on because I like it." I wonder why he likes it so much. Because it reminds him of a time he was scared but he did it anyway and now he feels like a winner. Nothing can buy that feeling. It can only come from being courageous yourself.

So, where does our courage come from? Courage comes from faith. Cicero, from 100 BC, said, "A man of courage is also full of faith." When life squeezes you, the real stuff comes out. The question is whether it is hope or despair? Are you filled with faith or fear? "Fear knocked at the door. Faith answered. And lo, no one was there." Replace your fear with faith. Faith comes from our beliefs. There are foundational beliefs that will greatly impact your level of faith and, therefore, your ability to fulfill your mission. Let's begin our pursuit by reviewing our belief system and the process by which we obtain results.

CHAPTER 13

The Process of Results

*The outer conditions of a person's life will always
be found to reflect their inner beliefs.*
–James Allen

Everything that happens to us in our life we process in our mind. When we are born, we begin life with a clear mind. It's like a brand-new computer — the operating system is installed but all the programs haven't been loaded yet. A baby is so fresh and pure. A new computer is without bugs or anything that can cause it to freeze up or even slow it down. Then, it all begins. You start loading up that computer with stuff and some of it allows you to do great things and some of it just bogs your system down and causes errors to occur. A baby immediately upon birth is exposed to a whole world of stimulation. As we grow, we take the things we experience and, based on the hard-wiring (i.e., that which actually makes the original computer) core values we hold, we assign meaning to the experience. This assignment creates a belief. And, the collection of our beliefs is known as our belief system.

As children we assign meaning as best as we can given our

small amount of wisdom we have to work with at that point in time. Consequently, as kids we may assign inaccurate meanings to our experiences. A sad example is when younger children observe violence between their parents and struggle to assign meaning to it. Often they simply conclude that they "must have done something wrong." This self-blaming belief can result in feelings of guilt, worry and anxiety. Since most young children do not have the ability to clearly verbalize their feelings, the only clue that such emotions are occurring is often through their behavior. They may become more withdrawn and regress to clinging and whining more.

As we continue to grow, we continue to assign meaning to more experiences, thereby growing our belief system. Our life is a direct result. The process is automatic. We experience something and we look to our belief system to reveal its meaning. Based on the revealed meaning, a feeling or set of feelings are triggered. These feelings produce a resulting attitude. It's our attitude that leads to our actions. Our actions lead to our results in life. Therefore, if we have accurate beliefs, then we can expect appropriate feelings, attitudes and actions to follow. If our beliefs are flawed (such as the self-blame of a child), an experience may well trigger inappropriate feelings with corresponding attitudes and actions leading to undesirable results. For example, one individual I have worked with told me that he was a "People Pleaser" (a common attitude). When I asked why he was a people pleaser, after great thought, he said, "I guess it is because as a little kid I was always getting into really big trouble for little things. My parents were really rough. It hurt — a lot. Consequently, as I grew up I wanted to avoid that pain and felt if I could just keep everyone happy around me then I'd be OK." So, a belief was established that said, "Please people to avoid pain." This belief led to a feeling of insecurity (fear of pain) and the attitude to please. Action was therefore always taken to please others even if it wasn't in his own best interest. The results are easy to imagine. He experienced the exact thing that he was attempting to avoid — pain. After years of negative results, he now learned that this particular belief is not a good one to maintain.

The results in our life are automatically compared to our operating beliefs. If the result supports the belief, then the belief becomes stronger, "more solid." If the result doesn't support the belief, then the belief becomes less compelling as noted in the last example. Unfortunately, often a flawed belief, such as, "I am not intelligent," will be supported every time you do something that appears unintelligent. For many of us, that could be all the time! This belief may have come from the comments of a teacher or a parent and, without correcting it, it will have a dramatic effect on our life. Specifically, our self-esteem would obviously be negatively affected which, in turn, would adversely affect every area of our life. Not only would one be much more hesitant to attempt things, but the low expectation would automatically lead to a lesser performance than one is capable of. A better belief which would be a good replacement could be, "My genius is unique to me." That is, I may not be very bright in one area but I have my own genius in another area. This belief will give us room to accept that we may not be smart in every way while leading us to search for where our true genius lives."

The following diagram illustrates the process:

Who We Are	Internal Thoughts & Feelings		External Actions & Results		Feedback to Thoughts
Core Values ➤	Belief System ➤ Emotions ➤	Attitude ➤	Actions ➤ Results	➤	Belief System

This diagram illustrates the process. Our core values define who we are and what we stand for. They are unchanging. When we experience something, our beliefs that we defined over the years, revel our perceived meaning of the event. Consequently, the determined meaning automatically triggers the appropriate feelings. These feelings support a particular attitude. Our attitude leads to the external action that we take. Our actions determine the results we experience in life. These results then act as feedback to our internal belief system, either increasing or lessening the belief's strength.

As a result, when people want to change the results in their life, the trap most people fall into is simply trying to change their actions without changing their thinking (i.e., their belief system and corresponding emotions and attitudes). Too often people just say, "I'm not going to act this way anymore." It certainly is a noble effort to do better. But, the reality is when you get tired or let your guard down, you'll default into the action that's naturally triggered by your emotion and attitude or that is simply habitual. The key is whenever possible work to modify your beliefs on something to let it change your corresponding emotions and watch your actions effortlessly align.

In this section, we will discuss each part of this process. First, we will take a deeper look at our core values to verify that they are truly real. Next, we will review systems to weed out faulty beliefs. Finally, we will take a close look at our emotions, attitudes and actions as well as processing our corresponding results. There are times when it is important to be able to operate starting at the emotional level. This topic is referred to as Emotional Intelligence. Sometimes we need to start with modifying our attitude. Additionally, we will also discuss concepts to maximize your effectiveness with your external actions. The result yields a complete arsenal of tools to work with to achieve the best overall results.

CHAPTER **14**

Are Your
Core Values Real?

*The world is full of people that have stopped listening
to themselves or have listened only to their neighbors
to learn what they ought to do, how they ought to
behave, and what the values are they should be living for.*
–Joseph Campbell

Are you really who you think you are? You've got to love
the question. It runs near the level of Descartes' phrase, "I
think therefore I am." Your core values define who you are
and what you stand for. But, have you incorrectly identified something as a core value that was actually a belief you
bought into? We'll call it a "Should-Value". That is, it is something you believe you should value because Simon says you
should. Identifying your Should-Values and making life adjustments accordingly will yield tremendous internal peace.
Whenever you are not "supporting yourself" you will feel internal conflict. For example, many people believe, "I should
make a certain amount of money," although they may have a
core value that believes they should do something they feel
has purpose, regardless of the money it pays. If that were

the case, can you see how difficult it may be to decide where to work? You may choose the job that pays more since that's what you think you "should" do but internally you feel conflicted and frustrated. You are never able to throw your heart into your work since your heart is telling you that you really belong somewhere else. This process is about peeling away what isn't really you so that you can clearly support your true self.

Although important, this task can be a bit scary as we are diving down to your core and taking a serious look around. When you do this and reveal some of the items you discover need removal or replacement, it can create some fear as to what the true you will look like in the end. Don't worry...believe it or not, the true you is beautiful and free. Cleaning anything can often seem overwhelming and even cause a little more mess at first. However, when the dust settles it's done — it feels great!

> *"Simonisms"(or "Shoulds") are things that others have informed you that you should accept as truth.*

Should-values (or "Shoulds" for short — we could also call them "Simonisms") are things that others have informed you that you "should" accept as truth. However, without realizing it, we adopt these Shoulds as part of our core values and belief system. Unfortunately, since they're not necessarily who we are or what we truly believe, they usually cause internal conflict. It comes down to supporting others' values and beliefs and not our own without even realizing it. There are three types of Shoulds: Having Shoulds, Doing Shoulds, and Being Shoulds.

Having Shoulds are things that others have convinced you that you should have. "Have" examples: a good job, a new car, a certain in-fashion look, and the latest and greatest whatevers.

Doing Shoulds are things that others have convinced you that you should do. "Do" examples: pursue a certain occupation, live in a certain area, act a particular way (like act your age), keep up with the news, and carry your cell phone 24/7. Being Shoulds are the most critical to be aware of. They consist of things that that others have convinced you that you should be. "Be" examples: beautiful, smart, funny, successful, well-connected, and perfect.

Being Shoulds are most critical and damaging because they encapsulate your being all of the time. You are allowing them to define you. If you believe you should be successful and you are not fitting that picture, now what? If you believe you should be perfect, what happens when you aren't? Not achieving what you believe you should have or do is bad enough, but not achieving who you believe you should be is unconscionable. As a result of not living up to "Being Shoulds," many people suffer from very low self worth and self esteem.

> *As a result of not living up to "Being Shoulds," many people suffer with very low self worth and self esteem.*

The idea of living by Should values happens naturally as we seek acceptance from others. The resulting challenge, however, is that by doing so we actually never get a chance to live our own life. Rather, we are living the life that others have defined for us. Further, we are never going to feel the peace of living according to our own self and our own purpose.

Watch what happens to the opinion you have of yourself when you rid yourself of your Should values and rate yourself according to living by your core values. Begin the process of allowing yourself to define you. Reflect on your Shoulds. What have you accepted as a Have Should, a Do Should, and most importantly a Be Should? Write them down. Seriously think about them. Then, write down the related value that you hold true.

To refer to an earlier example:

My Having Should:
I should have a good
paying job.

Value Statement:
Choose work that is most
in alignment with my
talents and my purpose.

My Having Shoulds: Value Statements:

_____   _____

_____   _____

_____   _____

My Doing Shoulds:

_____   _____

_____   _____

_____   _____

My Being Shoulds:

_____   _____

_____   _____

_____   _____

Another simple method for identifying Shoulds is to look at your list of core values and their corresponding ranking of importance from Section 2: *Discovering your Life Purpose*. Next to those rankings is a column titled, "Behavior." For each core value rank your behavior — how well you live your values — using the same scale of 1-5 (1=Don't live it at all, 3=Somewhat live it, 5=Live it all the time).

When you have completed ranking your behavior, look at the comparison between your earlier marked value ranking and your currently marked behavior ranking. Note any values that have a higher behavior ranking than value ranking. These values are more than not Should values rather than true values. That is, if you don't really value something but find you are doing it a lot, it is often a clue that your doing is based on something you feel you should do and not because you internally value it.

For example, let's say you gave "Personal Appearance" a value score of 2 yet you gave your behavior a score of 5 (i.e., you always are concerned about your personal appearance). These scores indicate that a Should value has been adopted as your actions are not driven by what you value but rather by external influences. This will certainly create internal conflict as your behavior and your *beliefs* are not in alignment.

> *Don't let people "should" on you!*

Once you have filled in the Behavior column, complete the process by writing down an appropriate action step each time you identify any behavior ranking that is higher than the value rankings. The action step is something that you can do to better align your behavior with the true degree of importance you place on the value.

> *When others tell you what you should do, compare it to your values to determine you will accept it or reject it.*

Regularly search for internal Shoulds and replace them with appropriate value statements. Once you have replaced your Shoulds with value statements, you no longer are living by others' standards but rather by what you value and believe. Then, from this point forward, don't let people "should" on you! When others tell you what you should do, compare it to your values to determine if you will accept it or reject it.

CHAPTER 15

Belief System Update

All personal breakthroughs begin with a change in beliefs.
–Anthony Robbins

BELIEF SYSTEM ➤ EMOTIONS ➤ ATTITUDE ➤ ACTIONS ➤ RESULTS

One of the very most important things that you can do is review and update your beliefs. Our beliefs are a funny thing. Although we are not even sure why we hold most of the beliefs that we do and often don't know where they came from, we all have a natural instinct to protect them. Like a mother protecting her young, we tend to vigorously guard our beliefs and hold them closely to us. We immediately feel defensive when they are challenged. Why do we naturally do this? Can you say, "Ego"? Our beliefs are held deep inside just outside our inner core (core valuess). Admitting we have been operating under a faulty belief is very close to admitting that our core is faulty. In addition, harder than admitting we did one thing wrong is admitting we had an incorrect thought process (belief) that led to numerous wrong results. Our egos don't like to admit that anything is wrong. However, it is essential to let your ego know that now isn't the time to get cranky. No guarding or blocking right now — it's time for some quality house cleaning. The pain of updating your beliefs is nothing compared to the beauty of a transformed life! So, stay strong through the process...for some I know you may dig into some uncomfortable areas that are not too pleasurable, but it will all be worth it. You can do this!

Once again, there are many methods available. This particular method to search for and update your beliefs is simple and effective. The heart of it is a matter of asking the key question, "Why?" enough times. That's it. Simple enough? Here's how it works:

Step 1: Begin with a result that wasn't positive.
Step 2: Begin asking, "why?" working back from the Result to the Belief.
Step 3: Once you've worked back to the root belief, confirm it isn't an effective belief for good results, determine a replacement for it and confirm why the replacement will be a better belief. Ask the remaining three questions to accomplish this:

- How's it been working for me?
- What would be a better belief to replace it?
- Why do you think that will be a better belief?

The following is a real example of an individual using this approach exactly:

What do you regret? Not finishing nursing school.
Why didn't you finish? I got married and moved.
Why didn't you finish at a different school? Too

much work to start over.

Why did you feel it was too much? It was easier to just quit.

Why do you believe that? I have always believed, if you don't like it then don't do it.

How's that belief been working for you? Not so well. I've quit everything.

What would be a better belief to replace that one with? Never quit. Give it your all.

Why do you think that will be a better belief? The reward of the extra effort of feeling proud and self-accomplished will far outweigh the feeling of regret by quitting.

Although the process isn't necessarily the most enjoyable, the results will transform your life! Take some time to identify some Results that weren't positive. Work back using the above process to identify the faulty belief. Finally, replace the belief with a new one. Use the area below to record your thoughts:

Negative Result	Faulty Belief	Replacement Belief

Another approach to identifying and updating your beliefs is to take notice of everything that's said in your head. This may sound absurd but you'll be shocked at what goes on in there when you really take time to consciously make note of it. Often, our beliefs are established and/or reinforced by accepting what's being said in our head. Unfortunately, for many, their self-talk (Simon chatter) is horrific. Not only would most people not be friends with anyone that talked to them that way but they would consider them a jerk or other such names. From the moment many people wake up there's almost nothing but negative banter going on in their internal boardroom. It is absolutely essential that two things happen with your self-talk: First, understand your role with it. Second, take control of it.

> *Understand that you're not the "talker" in your head, that's Simon. You're the "listener."*

The first major realization is to understand that you are not the "talker" in your head — that's Simon. You're the "listener." Hang with me; this goes a little deep. When something is said in our head, we naturally think that we "said" it, particularly because it's always in the first person — we consider it our thought. For example, you may mess up on something and suddenly in your head you "say." "I'm so stupid." However, you didn't say it. You heard it. In other words, it was said to you that "You are so stupid," but simply in the first-person context so that you own it. With this clarity, you now have the ability to accept or reject this input. Prior to being the listener, you would naturally accept it as fact without consideration because you thought you said it. This will wreck havoc on your self-worth and self-esteem, lending you much more vulnerable to accept minimizing beliefs.

Understanding that you are not the talker but rather the listener in your head yields an entirely new level of awareness. This "internal separation" immediately empowers you as you no longer are the unknowing victim of what is being said. It also identifies that fact that what is being said is not who you are but rather just something that you accepted as truth. This clarity is critical in order to have self-worth and in order for you to confidently choose to accept or reject what is being said in your head.

When stormy dialogue surrounds children they will often leave the room or even hide. As they hear parents arguing or worse, as they will be verbally attacked themselves, they attempt to retreat from it all. However, things change as we grow up. As it is said, "What was once outside becomes inside." The negative attacks and critical voices that we ran from as children suddenly aren't outside anymore but rather inside. Consequently, there is nowhere to hide. We hear critical voices and negative comments but there's no retreat. Unknowingly, we aren't separated from our thoughts and little by little we accept them as truth resulting in a cemented belief of who we are.

Taking control of what's happening in your head is a matter of three steps:

Step 1: Awareness. Be aware of what is being said in your head and realize that you are the listener and not the talker.

Step 2: Accept or Reject. As you "hear" what is being said in your head, simply accept it as true or reject it as false.

Step 3: Replace Negative with Positive. For everything you reject, replace it with something positive. This may be a positive affirmation or Scripture. For example, you may say, "I reject that comment that I am stupid. Rather, I can do all things through Christ, who strengthens me."

In order to trigger awareness to begin this process, give the following mental exercise a try. When you first wake up in the morning, start writing down everything that comes into your mind regarding self talk. Listen carefully and remember it is tricky because it comes in the form of first person. However, as you write everything out throughout the day, you will quickly improve. By the end of the day, see what comes out. The process will bring clarity as to what's being said in a typical day up there as well as begin to increase your awareness of what's happening. Once you're more aware of what is truly being said, you can then complete the other steps of accepting or rejecting and replacing the comments. Additionally, you can take a pro-active approach by planting positive seeds of affirmation or Scripture in addition to responding to what is happening in your head. Of course, that is just for those who want to be in the accelerated class.

KEY BELIEF: You were created by God

In addition to identifying and updating our beliefs in general, there is one belief that I would like to suggest for serious consideration. That is: You were created by God. We all want our life to have value, meaning and purpose regardless of our economic status, race or religion. It is one of the few things we all really do have in common. Everyone wants to feel their life made sense with meaning. Deep down we all want it to count for something. However, in order to discover and fulfill our purpose, we must have one. In order to have a purpose, we must know that God exists and created us. If there isn't a God, then you were not designed; since there isn't a designer (meaning you were not designed) then you have no specific purpose or meaning. You are simply a spatial thing; a happenstance of the environment — a highly evolved amoeba which developed from nothingness.

If it is true that you exist and were not created by God, then the good news is you don't need to read the rest of this book! What's the point? No purpose means there's no need for you to search for one. In fact, if that were the case, then why a moral code at all? If you are just heading back to dust without an eternal life following your death, then you best enjoy everything to your greatest satisfaction while you can. Don't worry about others since there is no accountability for your actions. You may say, "I can determine my own purpose even if I were such a happenstance." That is, you can find something that you can make a difference with even if you weren't designed for anything specific. Perhaps you can. I'm all for random acts of kindness or meaningful work. However, my question back to you would be why would it really matter? If after your life you are just heading into the abyss of nothingness along with everyone else, then obviously nothing you do really has any lasting value. If you argue that point, saying somehow you could contribute some lasting value, then I would ask you where does the feeling of wanting to do so come from? If your existence really comes from simply "survival of the fittest," then caring and contribution aren't aligning values. Rather, these values are polar opposite of the survival practices of natural selection.

In addition, it is important to understand the difference between purpose and meaning. Meaning, as we discussed regarding the development of our belief system, is significance you attach to an event, person or situation. You can have meaningful work if you decide to assign meaning to it. For example, there were three masons cutting stone. When the first was asked what he was doing, he replied, "I'm cutting stone." When the second was asked, he replied, "I'm earning a living." When the third was asked, he replied, "I'm building a cathedral." Here three men are doing the same job. Yet, they are doing the job having assigned various degrees of meaning to it.

The assignment of meaning to what you do is very important. It will make a big difference in your life and the enjoyment you experience. However, the assignment of meaning to events in life alone doesn't necessarily mean you are living a life on purpose. A meaningful life doesn't necessarily mean it fulfilled your purpose. However, a life that fulfills your purpose will necessarily also be meaningful.

I've noticed that every atheist I have ever met is angry. I don't blame them, I would be angry too. After all, in an atheist's world, we weren't designed for a purpose and we all know how our story ends — it is the worst-case scenario — we end into nothingness for eternity. What's worse, there is nothing whatsoever that we can do about it. How awful! One atheist said, "I'm not angry. I'm unsettled." I would say they are rightfully unsettled which is actually the source of their anger. I would also be tremendously fearful, given at any moment something could happen to me and it's over. Really over. How scary is that?

Most people just avoid the subject of God. Whatever you

do, "Don't talk about religion or politics," we've all been told. "It makes people uncomfortable." Yes, why talk about our maker, our destiny, and our laws that govern our time here on earth? I know, we don't want to mention anything controversial. Even more so, we don't want to make anyone uncomfortable by encouraging them to explore the thought of what will happen to them when they die (In fact, we don't even like to say, "die" or "dead" but tend towards, "deceased," "departed," "passed on" or something less direct). It is interesting to me how families will spend countless hours discussing and planning a vacation but avoid any dialog about their journey upon death.

> *Wouldn't you agree that eternity is the wrong thing to be wrong about?*

Which trip do you suppose will last longer? Which will be more significant? Wouldn't you agree that eternity is the wrong thing to be wrong about?

I strongly encourage you to solidify your belief in God as well as your beliefs about God. Know what you believe and know why you believe it. Then seek not just to know about God, but to actually know God. There is a big difference. As you seek a closeness with your creator, you will have begun your journey towards understanding His purpose for you. Start in prayer. Then, commit a lifetime to seek His wisdom.

> *As you seek a closeness with your creator, you will have begun your journey towards understanding His purpose for you.*

Once we agree that you were created by a Creator, then we can conclude that there is a specific purpose He had in mind for you. The next step is to have faith in God that He wants to see your success. There is a saying, "Stuff happens." Ok, maybe you have heard another version. Regardless, life is difficult. Open up any newspaper and start reading. It's not all rosy, is it? Death, divorce, accidents, lies, manipulation,...it's all in there, daily. There is no denying it and nobody is exempt. As Sheri Barr said, "Expecting life to treat you well because you are a good person is like expecting an angry bull not to charge because you are a vegetarian."

> *"Expecting life to treat you well because you are a good person is like expecting an angry bull not to charge because you are a vegetarian."*
> *-Sheri Barr*

So, how can we stay the course in the pursuit of our mission when tough times attack our life? Faith. Once again, it comes back to faith. Your Creator, the same Creator who created the universe, is there to see you through it. Do you really think that God is looking at your problem and saying, "Man, I don't know...this is a tough one. I could put the universe together, create heaven and earth and everything in it, but how can I help you get through the loss of your job? I just don't know..." I'm not trying to make light of any tough situation, there really is pain and true problems in the world. However, my point isn't to diminish your problems but rather help you enlarge your perspective of God.

> *How could you really pursue your God-given purpose without faith in God to see you though?*

And, although this book isn't designed to preach, it is designed to get you to think. How could you really pursue your God-given purpose without faith in God to see you though?

We've all heard people say it, "Well, you know...everything happens for a reason," as they attempt to give comfort during a troubling time. Yes, everything happens for a reason; it was a result of someone exercising their free will. That isn't the amazing part. The amazing part is that God has the ability to take the bad in your life and turn it to good for His purpose for you. Have you ever noticed, looking back on your life, that tragedies were actually turning points used for good? We all have experiences that we can think about in hindsight. "Who would have known that if [ABC] didn't happen then [XYZ] wouldn't be the case now?" is the kind of talk you hear regularly. Looking back on our life and feeling peace from making sense of things is most often a lot easier than feeling peace during a conflict because you know there will be a good reason for it. In other

> *Life makes sense looking backwards but the struggle is to live with faith moving forward.*

words, life makes sense looking backwards but the struggle is to live with faith moving forward. However, if you will take the time to review the many conflicts that have occurred in your life and what positive came as a result, you will be able to grow your faith and feel a stronger sense of peace during present-day challenges.

Consider the following fable by author Orrin Woodward about a King and his friend:

An African king had a close friend who had the habit of remarking "this is good" about every occurrence in life no matter what it was. One day the king and his friend were out hunting. The king's friend loaded a gun and handed it to the king, but alas he loaded it wrong and when the king fired it, his thumb was blown off.

"This is good!" exclaimed his friend.

The horrified and bleeding king was furious. "How can you say this is good? This is obviously horrible!"

he shouted.

The king put his friend in jail.

About a year later the king went hunting by himself. Cannibals captured him and took him to their village. They tied his hands, stacked some wood, set up a stake and bound him to it. As they came near to set fire to the wood, they noticed that the king was missing a thumb. Being superstitious, they never ate anyone who was less than whole. They untied the king and sent him on his way.

Full of remorse, the king rushed to the prison to release his friend.

"You were right, it WAS good" the king said.

The king told his friend how the missing thumb saved his life and added, "I feel so sad that I locked you in jail. That was such a bad thing to do."

"NO! This is good!" responded his delighted friend.

"Oh, how could that be good, my friend, I did a terrible thing to you while I owe you my life".

"It is good," said his friend, "because if I wasn't in jail I would have been hunting with you and they would have killed ME."

"This is good" makes sense when enough time can pass so that we may finally learn what God has known all along. It is when we try to play God and create our own purpose with our own plan that we end up frustrated, tired and dejected. Ever hear the saying, "If you want to make God laugh, tell him your plans!"? It is not that we shouldn't make plans — of course we should. We should just make them according to His will for our life (since He's the Creator) and be flexible to change if necessary knowing that we don't know what only God knows.

The real question is can you say "This is good," during the tough time *prior* to understanding how it worked out for you? It is about having faith. Given God made you for a purpose and has a plan for your life, can you have faith in Him? A powerful verse in the Bible says, "And we know that in all things God works for the good of those who love him, who have been called according to his purpose." (Romans 8:28) Your degree of peace during difficulties reveals your faith. Imagine the peace you would feel with the security of knowing that the God of the universe has your best interest in mind. It's like seeing a movie for the second time and knowing all along how well it all works out in the end. It's a lot more relaxing, isn't it?

How can God make good come from bad when we have the freedom to choose our own actions as does everyone else? It is that soft-still voice. It is our intuition. It is the ideas that pop into our mind. Yes, some of our intuition can be the power of our unconscious mind, yet, there are times when we are given insights that we can choose to act upon that could only have come from God. How many times have you found yourself saying, "What a coincidence!" or "What are the odds of this happening?!" Is it really a coincidence or is it more of a divine appointment with something or someone? As the saying goes, "Coincidence is when God chooses to remain anonymous." How did God make certain people's paths cross? What did he put in their heart to encourage them to choose to be at a certain place or do or say a certain something at just the right time? The details are for God to know. Attempting to know all the details or to go any further in thought such as asking where God came from is futile. As Rick Warren put it so well in a Newsweek article, April 9, 2007, "Trying to understand where God came from is like an ant trying to understand the Internet."

The following was organized by an anonymous author regarding Little Things. It is regarding how a few mostly "unplanned" little things kept people alive in New York City on Sept. 11, 2001:

Little Things

The head of a company survived 9/11 because his son started kindergarten.

Another gentleman is alive because it was his turn to bring donuts.

One woman was late because her alarm clock didn't go off in time.

One was late because of being stuck on the NJ Turnpike due to an auto accident.

One missed his bus.

One spilled food on her clothes and had to take time to change.

One's car wouldn't start.

One went back to answer the telephone.

One had a child that dawdled and didn't get ready as soon as he should have.

One couldn't hail a taxi.

One put on a new pair of shoes that morning but, before he got to work, developed a blister on his foot. He stopped at a drugstore to buy a Band-Aid. That is why he is alive today.

Now when I am stuck in traffic, miss an elevator, turn back to answer a ringing telephone ... all the little things that could annoy any of us, I think to myself, "This is exactly where God wants me to be at this very moment..." Next time your morning seems to be going wrong — the children are slow getting dressed, you can't seem to find the car keys, and you hit every traffic light — be grateful; God is at work watching over you. May God continue to bless you with all those annoying little things and may you remember their possible purpose.

-anonymous

Some people believe in God but truly lack faith because they see too much unexplained suffering in the world. They will say things like, "How can God allow (or cause) such suffering?" "How can I have faith in a God like that?" The truth is suffering is a result of our sin. Our sin is a result of our choices. We may be tempted, but it is our choice to act on that temptation. Our sinful actions ultimately hurt others. There is an unlimited number of ways for this to happen. If it is not an obvious hurt directly to someone then it may likely support something that in turn is hurting someone. It may set a negative cycle in motion that will hurt someone, etc. How is all this connected? Stay with me. If God were not to allow evil to happen, then He would have to stop our freedom of choice. Our free will is God's great blessing and curse that He gave us. We have the free will to choose our actions. If we didn't, then we really wouldn't be living. Rather, we would simply be puppets with strings attached to the hands of God. We would merely be an extension of His imagination. We certainly wouldn't have a purpose to fulfill anymore than does a doll laying on your child's bedroom floor. We would be more like a programmed robot sent to earth. A program has prede-termined functionality — if this...then that... No, we are not puppets with strings nor are we programmed robots walking the earth. We are living, thinking and personally responsible beings. We exercise our free will to act and, consequently due to our poor choices, the world is no longer a perfect place.

What is awe-inspiring, however, as noted earlier is re-gardless of how bad our choices are and those of the people around us — regardless of the mess that we may have made of life — God can ultimately use it all for our good. It is during these difficult times that our character is developed in such a way that we obtain the ability to fulfill our purpose. How amazing is that? God will take our struggles and use them for our strength. Helen Keller said, "Character cannot be developed in ease and quiet. Only through experi-ence of trial and suffering can the soul

> "Character cannot be developed in ease and quiet. Only through experience of trial and suffering can the soul be strengthened, vision cleared, ambition inspired, and success achieved."
> —Helen Keller

be strengthened, vision cleared, ambition inspired, and suc-cess achieved." Gothe simply said, "Character develops itself in the stream of life." Ironically, struggles are necessary to achieve greatness. Just as a butterfly must go through the struggle of freeing itself from its cocoon in order to develop the strength to fly, we too must grow from our struggles in order to fulfill our mission.

WISDOM, EMPATHY, & PASSION

Specifically, our struggles will provide lessons to develop wisdom, pain to develop empathy, and drama to spark the passion of purpose. Wisdom, empathy and passion are all necessary ingredients of a person of character.

Wisdom

Have you ever heard someone say, "I learned it from the school of hard knocks"? Well, the reality of life is that we are all enrolled in this school. Some people are simply doing better than others in learning their lessons. Have you ever noticed that when someone has a life lesson that they fail to learn, life tends to repeat the lesson? Remember, your lesson is there for a reason. Learn it. The goal is to avoid repeating the same grade! There's a saying, "Dog bites me once — shame on dog. Dog bites me twice — shame on me." Often during troubled times, people don't focus on God's plan for them and revert to saying, "Oh, why me?" If you want to move off the lesson, then don't ask, "Why?" ask, "What?" That is, ask, "What am I supposed to learn? What is my lesson in this?" There is a story of a man who was asked how he became so successful. He said, "By making a lot of wise decisions." When asked where he gained the wisdom to make so many wise decisions he responded, "By making a lot of unwise decisions." Life's tough lessons bring us wisdom.

Empathy

Nobody of sound mind likes to endure pain. However, it too is a necessary component of growth. Empathy is intellectually identifying with another's feelings, thoughts or attitudes. The challenge is without a similar experience of your own, you can, at best, sympathize with them. However, having a personal experience of your own that can be recalled in order to relate with another's situation is powerful. There is no greater way to deeply connect with someone. Abraham Lincoln understood the power of empathy and once remarked, "Whenever I hear anyone arguing for slavery, I feel a strong impulse to see it tried on him personally." Yes, empathy can be powerful.

On an early December morning before the sun began to rise, I was amongst a group of swimmers enduring a very cold morning practice. It was dark, windy, rainy, and, most importantly, freezing as the heaters had gone out during the night, leaving the water frigid cold. We were miserable. Although we were some of the nation's top swimmers, during this morning's practice we all whined and complained like never before. Our coach Mike Troy kept telling us we were fine, but to no avail. Then, it happened. One of the greatest examples of empathizing that I have ever witnessed. He looked as us all and said, "You guys are really cold, aren't you? You are miserable? You are suffering?" Then, without saying another word and while holding his umbrella upright, he walked to the edge of the pool and continued right in! That's right, he walked right into the pool fully clothed — raincoat and all. Standing chest high in the water (and still holding his umbrella) he looked as us all and said, "Okay, now we are all in the same boat. You're right, it's cold. Now, can we continue with the rest of

> *The best way to help someone is to follow the two step process: Connect and Lead.*

practice?" We all looked around dumbfounded and simultaneously said, "Yea, coach." He continued to walk up and down the pool in that freezing cold water holding his umbrella and shouting out encouragement as we swam.

The best way to help someone is to follow the two-step process: Connect and Lead. Therapy, or any attempt to help someone, must start with a connection. Too often people try to lead others without connecting first. The process of giving someone advice, attempting to motivate them or direct them in any way is ineffective because trust has not yet been established. Trust begins by someone feeling understood. There is an old saying, "People don't care what you know until they know that you care." People feel understood when you can empathize with them. Given the connection, you are now in a position to lead them to a better place.

Passion

Life's struggles, therefore, are necessary. They give you the ability to connect with empathy and build trust and understanding. They also give you the wisdom you need in order to make wise decisions and lead others once a connection has been made. However, as important as these benefits are, without passion they would be of no value. Best put by author Greg Olson, "Ignorance on fire is better than knowledge on ice." What is the point to gain wisdom and the ability to empathize if you don't have the passion to apply it to your purpose?

I heard someone recently say, "This nation is filled with couch-potatoes that are starting to give birth to tater tots." The drama of life will spark the passions that connect with your purpose. Have you ever witnessed some dramatic event only to

The purpose of certain events for you is simply to spark the passion of your own purpose.

notice that you were passionately moved while others didn't feel the connection? The greatest of blazes started with the first spark. The purpose of certain events for you is simply to spark the passion of your own purpose. Drama in your life most certainly is uncomfortable but notice what sparks fly and be open to where it may ignite and lead you.

> *Pray not for an easier life, pray to be a bigger person.*

Given the value that can come from our challenges, is it going too far to be grateful for them? Perhaps that would be over the top; even if they are necessary. "I'm so happy for this problem" — probably not. But, we can be grateful in our challenges for a God that has a plan to use it for our good. Pray not for an easier life, pray to be a bigger person. The bottom line: let's learn to say, "This is good."

CHAPTER 16

Emotional Intelligence

*It is very important to understand that emotional intelligence is
not the opposite of intelligence, it is not the triumph of heart over
head — it is the unique intersection of both.*
–David Caruso

> BELIEF SYSTEM ➤ **EMOTIONS** ➤ ATTITUDE ➤ ACTIONS ➤ RESULTS

Improving the quality of your belief system is the method
for long-lasting, improved results. However, there are times
when you need to address life directly from an emotional
standpoint. The more effective you are with regards to working with emotions, the greater our results in life will be. As
stated by Ayman Sawaf, "Learning how to become emotionally literate is one of the best investments that human beings
can make for themselves, their children, and the future."

Having the ability to manage your emotions is actually
part of a science commonly referred to as Emotional Intelligence. Emotional Intelligence (EI), often measured as an
Emotional Intelligence Quotient (EQ), describes an ability,
capacity or skill to perceive, assess, and manage the emotions of one's self, of others and of groups. As a fairly new area

of psychological research, the definition of EI is constantly changing. However, it generally includes the following abilities as described in Daniel Goleman's 1998 book, "Working with Emotional Intelligence."

1. Self-awareness — the ability to read one's emotions and recognize their impact while using gut feelings to guide decisions.

2. Self-management — involves controlling one's emotions and impulses and adapting to changing circumstances.

3. Social awareness — the ability to sense, understand and react to other's emotions while comprehending social networks.

4. Relationship management — the ability to inspire, influence and develop others while managing conflict.

The success and significance of your life will be directly related to how well you work with others. There is simply no way around it. Your purpose will have to do with other people and the higher your EQ, the tighter your connection will be with them. Studying and understanding the science of Emotional Intelligence and raising your personal Emotional Quotient is one of the greatest self-development focuses you can have. Each of the four areas above is a science to study in and of itself. It is not only critical to develop the awareness and management of emotions within yourself, but

> *The success and significance of your life will be directly related to how well you work with others.*

also with regards to others around you. Let's look at couple of various aspects of Emotional Intelligence.

I regularly hear people say, "He/She made me so mad." While I will agree that they may have been rude or mean or downright nasty, they didn't make you anything. You chose your response. Oh, I know this one doesn't sit well right away but it is vitally important for you to understand. "He spit on me and that made me mad," you say. No, his spitting on you didn't make you mad, it made you slimy wet. You processed the meaning of his spitting on you and, as a result of your belief system, you concluded such that anger was the emotional result. What if our culture taught that you only spat on someone when you really respected them and wanted to honor them? If that was the culture and it was solidly implanted in your beliefs, then you would be thankful for the exact same event. So, the spitting didn't make you mad, but rather your processing of it is what led to your recently hydrated anger emotion. Do you get it? Yes, I know that is not what spitting means in our culture but according to whom? Who says you can't rewrite the rules of what things mean and re-establish how much value you should assign to them? For example, I find it helpful to raise the value of a person's actions according to the degree I respect them. In other words, if you don't respect someone, then their actions should carry less weight. I've seen my dad smile while driving and when I asked him what was up he'd say something like, "The guy behind us is waving at me but he's only using one finger," or "The guy behind us is telling me that I'm No. 1." My dad didn't know the person and simply noted his immature actions. Consequently, my dad's lack of respect for the individual could therefore decrease the value he placed on the man's hostility. And, by changing the meaning of something, he was able to smile and feel emotionally happy when otherwise he may have encountered some less enjoyable feeling. The bottom line is you get to choose! Can you do it? Imagine a life where your emotions don't have to be at the mercy of your environment. How awesome! The flip side of that is once you understand this, now it is your responsibility to choose well; you can't pass the buck off to others as the victim anymore. I admit it's a paradigm shift but that's what personal growth is all about. Remember, it's dream, struggle and then the victory. Rather than to dive too deeply into the subject, let me simply recommend that you make a lifelong commitment to this area of growth. And, always keep in mind the words of Charles Nalin, "Don't argue with a fool. The spectators can't tell the difference."

A couple of years ago, I raced into a post office to mail a package. I ran to the counter in a bit of a hurry, eager to complete my task. However, it wasn't to be so simple. The mail lady informed me that I needed to take a number and "step back behind the red line." I looked around and I was dumbfounded. The lady repeated, "Take a number, sir." I looked at her, smiled, took a number and retreated back to the little red line.

> "Don't argue with a fool. The spectators can't tell the difference."
> -Charles Nalin

The reason I was so confused was that she and I were the only two people in the post office! Next, she began to call out numbers..."Number 71?" she said, looking around as if there was actually a room full of people. "Number 72?" she continued. I stood there looking at my number in disbelief — my ticket read number 94. "Number 73?" she said followed by her standard look around. "She's got to be kidding," I remember thinking to myself. "Am I on a reality Candid Camera-type television show right now?" I thought. Even though I was in a hurry, I actually didn't say anything because now I was curious as to whether she was really going to read every successive number. She did. Then my big moment came. "Number 94," she said. "Oh, that's me!" I blurted out as if to speak over the noisy crowd. I walked up to the window expecting her to say something cute like, "Got ya!" However, she didn't miss a beat as she simply continued in character, "Hi. How may I help you?" I suddenly realized that this woman was dead serious. She wasn't joking at all.

We handled getting postage on my package and then before I left I knew I needed to say something. So, I did. "Ma'am, I've been going to the post office for many years," I began. "I have met many people who did what you do here. However, in all the years I have never seen anyone, anywhere care so much about following proper procedure. It is obvious that you really care about quality and doing things right." I said it because it was true. Not too many years earlier, however, I would never have considered acknowledging her — especially considering how odd it all was. In fact, I would have been upset and felt disrespected by her ridiculous waste of my time.

Yes, focusing on improving your emotional intelligence will make a significant impact on your life and, typically, it will make life much more enjoyable for you and everyone around you. The words no sooner left my mouth when I could see a nearly instantaneous effect. She was emotional and grateful as she said, "Yes, it is very important to me and I really try to do things by the book." The reality of the situation was that she was just doing her job as best as she could. Excellence and accuracy were key values for her — to say the least. So, it wasn't about what I value (Respect) but rather what she valued (Excellence) that created this most unusual experience. That is, she wasn't doing anything TO me (disrespecting me); she was doing something FOR herself (performing excellence, as she saw it). Had I become emotionally upset from disrespect it would have been an inaccurate assessment of the situation. A key understanding that will immediately improve your EQ is taught by Dr. Robert Rohm in his book, "Positive Personality Profiles": "People don't do things TO you, they do things FOR themselves."

> *"People don't do things TO you, they do things FOR themselves."*
> —Dr. Robert Rohm

Before we leave the topic, here is a quick pop quiz: You are driving home in your brand-new dream car. Suddenly, you hear a loud bang coming off your right car door. You look in your side-view mirror only to see one of the young neighborhood boys standing on the curb. You realize he just threw a large rock and it slammed into the side of your perfect car. Alright, how are you feeling? Mad? Disgusted? What do you do? Most people would stop, back up and confront the boy. Let's say you do. However, when you back up and park the car, the boy starts to run off over a mound of dirt behind the curb. You look at your new car and your door has a big dent in it. Do you follow him? A survey done with over 1,000 people concluded that more than half the people would follow the boy. However, when you catch up to the boy he stops, looks at you and says, "I'm so sorry, mister. Look! My brother was riding his bike when he fell and now he's unconscious. I couldn't get anyone to stop and help me so I had to throw the rock. I'm sorry. Please help my brother." Looking over, you do indeed see his brother lying on the ground, not moving. How do you feel now? Are you still mad or disgusted?

Isn't it amazing how quickly our emotions and, therefore, our attitude can instantly change? Now, let me ask you — what caused the change? The situation was the same all along. The only thing that changed was your understanding of all the facts. What if you didn't stop and just drove home in anger? Once home, you tell your spouse about how terrible the little rascal was and what a bad influence he is on the surrounding neighborhood. Your dialog leads to transferred anger in your spouse who, in turn, shares it with others. Rumors begin to fly and damage is done. One of the simplest lessons to learn in order to begin raising your EQ is to not jump to conclusions.

Remember long-time radio personality Paul Harvey? He would get a newspaper and read a story, sharing the facts as they were written. Then he would pause and say his famous line, "And now for the rest of the story," adding facts and commentary that wasn't included in the original story. Once he finished, the listeners had a whole new understanding of what it was all about. Remember that line, and the possibility there is more to the story when events transpire, and you will raise your EQ instantly. Combine that with the reminder that God can use the bad in our life for good and you will change your life.

Increasing your EQ is not an overnight project. It is not a matter of simply reading more books on the topic. Increasing your EQ is a process. It's about gaining more knowledge and regularly applying it. However, the rewards of internal peace along with the development of highly effective relationships will be well worth your effort.

The Cookie Thief

A woman was waiting at an airport one night,
With several long hours before her flight.
She hunted for a book in the airport shops.
Bought a bag of cookies and found a place to drop.
She was engrossed in her book but happened to see,
That the man sitting beside her, as bold as could be.
Grabbed a cookie or two from the bag in between,
Which she tried to ignore to avoid a scene.
So she munched the cookies and watched the clock,
As the gutsy cookie thief diminished her stock.
She was getting more irritated as the minutes ticked by,
Thinking, "If I wasn't so nice, I would blacken his eye."
With each cookie she took, he took one too,
When only one was left, she wondered what he would do.
With a smile on his face, and a nervous laugh,
He took the last cookie and broke it in half.
He offered her half, as he ate the other,
She snatched it from him and thought... oooh, brother.
This guy has some nerve and he's also rude,
Why he didn't even show any gratitude!
She had never known when she had been so galled,
And sighed with relief when her flight was called.
She gathered her belongings and headed to the gate,
Refusing to look back at the thieving ingrate.
She boarded the plane, and sank in her seat,
Then she sought her book, which was almost complete.
As she reached in her baggage, she gasped with surprise,
There was her bag of cookies, in front of her eyes.
If mine are here, she moaned in despair,

The others were his, and he tried to share.
Too late to apologize, she realized with grief,
That she was the rude one, the ingrate, the thief.

by Valerie Cox

How many times in our lives, have we absolutely
known that something was a certain way, only to discover
later that what we believed to be true ... was not?

CHAPTER 17

Attitude

*The greatest revolution of our generation is the discovery that
human beings, by changing the inner attitudes of their minds,
can change the outer aspects of their lives.*
–William James, US Pragmatist philosopher & psychologist

BELIEF SYSTEM ➤ EMOTIONS ➤ **ATTITUDE** ➤ ACTIONS ➤ RESULTS

In addition to directly accessing your emotions, it is also
important to directly affect your attitude. Your attitude is
everything. It will have tremendous impact on your success
and ultimate significance. Think of a couple of people that
you know that you truly admire. Take a moment and think
of a few of their qualities that have led you to admire them.
Really take a moment to think about it. Quickly write down
some of their qualities:

———————————————————

———————————————————

———————————————————

———————————————————

———————————————————

Most likely you wrote things like: Motivated, Positive, Honest, High Integrity, Humble, Caring, etc. Now, let me inquire, are these qualities based on an attitude or a skill? They all yield from an attitude, don't they? One chooses to be motivated, to have a positive attitude, to be humble and so on. Odds are the qualities that you wrote down were based primarily on attitudes as well; which goes to show you how important your attitude really is in your life. Are you going to choose to be positive or negative? Easy answer, you think? Well, I'm not talking about your attitude when things are going great. I'm talking about your attitude during times of transition or turbulence in your life. During these times, your attitude is tested and your character is revealed. Although there are countless attitudes that are of paramount importance, there are a few core attitudes that lead to many others:

1. Attitude of Gratitude — Regardless of what you are doing, maintaining an attitude of gratitude will produce a humble spirit and give you the proper perspective on life. It will allow you to remain gentle, peaceful and positive in times of challenge.

2. Attitude of Hunger — A hungry attitude will unveil resources, knowledge and energy. It will give you the motivation to maintain needed persistence to see you through.

3. Attitude of Possibility Thinking — An attitude of possibility thinking will take the lid off of your life. Too often we put limitations on ourselves as we focus on our own shortcomings. Rather, an attitude of possibility thinking will take the focus off of yourself and put it onto God. What is possible with God as your partner? Impossibility + God =

Miracle. An attitude of possibility thinking allows you to see and cast an inspiring vision.

ATTITUDE OF GRATITUDE

Have an attitude of gratitude. Get a checkup from the neck up. Take that frown and turn it around. Alright, enough already. You get it. You see, once we agree that you were created by a Creator, that there is a specific purpose He has in mind for you, and He is there to help you all the way, then we really have a lot to be grateful for. It is humbling when you really think about it and, in fact, an attitude other than that of gratitude means we have lost focus on the big picture of life and have tripped over our ego and our negative thoughts. Remember the King's friend, even during adversity, "This is good." Be grateful for your purpose and a God who wisely watches over you.

When you squeeze a banana, does orange juice pour out? When you squeeze a tomato do you find apple juice? Of course not. When you squeeze something, the real thing comes out. That is, what's really inside really comes out. Amazing isn't it? Well, here's a better question: When you are squeezed, what comes out? Let the question just sit for a moment... When you are squeezed, what comes out? You see, adversity doesn't develop character, it reveals it. Does your answer put a smile on your face or is it concerning? When squeezed, does love come out? Anger? Compassion? What are you so filled with that it is what must come out? OK, some of you may not like the answer. But, no worries, if you want something different to come out,

> *When you are squeezed, what comes out? You see, adversity doesn't develop character, it reveals it.*

then simply start filling yourself up with something new and better.

A person with a **harsh/cutting tongue** reveals
an **angry heart.**
A person with a **negative tongue** reveals
a **fearful heart.**
A person with a **boasting tongue** reveals
an **insecure heart.**
A person with a **judgmental tongue** reveals
a **guilty heart.**
A person with a **critical tongue** reveals
a **bitter heart.**
A person with a **filthy tongue** reveals
an **impure heart.**
A person with an **encouraging tongue** reveals
a **happy heart.**
A person with a **gentle tongue** reveals
a **loving heart.**
A person with a **loving/controlling of words tongue**
reveals a **peaceful heart.**

— Rick Warren

There is a story told by author John Maxwell in his book, *Think on These Things--Meditations for Leaders*, that illustrates this point. In his own words:

"Several years ago I read a true story...For four decades East Berlin was controlled by the Communists. West Berlin was free. One day some people who lived in East Berlin took a truckload of garbage and dumped it on the West Berlin side. The people of West Berlin could have retaliated by doing the same thing. But instead they took a truckload of canned goods, bread, and milk and neatly stacked it on the East Berlin side. On top of this stack of food they placed the sign: 'Each gives what he has.'"

One of the most important things you can choose to fill up with is Gratitude. Gratitude will manifest as patience, peace, love, compassion and humility. It will change the way you interpret the world and everything in it. Gratitude begins with faith and is obtained by reframing the way you see things. One perspective may lead to pride while another perspective regarding the same situation can lead to gratitude. It's all a matter of your perspective and it is your choice to decide.

"There but for the grace of God, go I." This quotation, expressing that someone's misfortune could easily have happened to oneself or anyone at all, is commonly traced back to the British Protestant reformer John Bradford (b. 1510 - d. 1555). He is said to have made the remark, "There but for the grace of God, go John Bradford," upon seeing criminals on their way to execution. He chose not to be prideful but rather humble due to his perspective that if it wasn't for the grace of God, it could well have been himself on his way to an early death. **Can you get there mentally or are you certain that if you lived their life it still wouldn't be you?** It's difficult to be arrogant when you are grateful for grace. He also understood that he can still stand up for the principles he believes in while feeling humble rather than prideful towards those who have fallen short of the mark. Martin Luther King, Jr. said, "He who you will change, you must first love." Have discord with actions but love people. Be grateful

> *Have discord with actions but love people.*

for God's grace.

Be grateful for what you have been given rather than upset over what you don't have or feel has been taken from you. What you have has been gifted to you. Count your blessings. Be grateful. All too often people complain: "I don't have enough money." "My home is a mess." "My kids are tiring." "There's nothing to eat in this house." "I'm not in good enough shape."

> Don't try to "stuff" your feelings but rather change the perspective and your feelings will follow.

Have you ever heard people say these things? I'm sure they're all true and, therefore, the feelings behind them are valid. However, if we want things to be better in our life we must learn to reframe them; put things into a different context. Don't try to "stuff" your feelings but rather change the perspective and your feelings will follow. To feel gratitude, change the perspective from looking at your situation from someone who is worse off than you. "I don't have enough money." Consider: Some people don't have any money at all. "My home is a mess." Consider: Millions of people are homeless. "My kids are tiring." Consider: Countless number of people want kids but can't have any. They would gladly be a tired parent. "There's nothing good to eat in this house." Consider: Millions of people are starving to death and could only dream of your last meal. "I'm not in good enough shape." Consider: Millions of people are battling cancer, AIDS and other bodily diseases.

If you truly focus on this new perspective even when you "don't feel like it," you will notice the release of tension and a new attitude of gratitude will come over you. I know it can be hard because when we don't feel happy we don't feel like changing a perspective on anything. But, remember, your victory comes from growing through your struggles. Now, don't misunderstand, I'm not advocating not caring about improving your situation. In fact, it is often necessary to come to a point of not being willing to tolerate a situation as it is anymore in order to ignite the action of change and improvement. So, by all means, improve those areas of life that you are passionate about. However, I am suggesting that all the while you can always choose a perspective that fosters an attitude of gratitude.

We have all heard the saying, "I felt sorry that I had no shoes, until I met a man with no feet." Great quote. Do you regularly apply it? Are you grateful for what you do have or do you take it for granted forever stuck in the habit of throwing regular pity parties for yourself? Although popular, those are expensive parties. Choose to see life through a grateful lens and, as a result, you will be able to celebrate while others commiserate. Recently, an elderly friend said, "I'm just grateful that wrinkles don't hurt." Yes, with the right perspective, you can always find something for which you can be grateful! Simply, "Life isn't about how to survive the storm, but how to dance in the rain." Will it make a difference in your life and in your pursuit towards fulfilling your Life Mission? Absolutely! Watch how an attitude of gratitude will draw key people closer to you along with more things for which to be grateful.

> *"Life isn't about how to survive the storm, but how to dance in the rain."*

Consider if you have kids, what do you feel when they are complaining that they don't have this or that? Do you feel a sense of urgency to get it for them or do you feel frustrated or unappreciated for what you have provided? How do you suppose God feels about you? Your life and everything in it has been a gift to you. But, have you worked hard for everything? I'm sure you have. But, where did your ambition come from? It's all a gift. Be grateful even for the little things. A man was running late to a job interview and trying to park his car. He prayed, "God please give me a parking spot so I can make this interview." Just then, a car starts to pull out. Immediately the man says, "Oh, never mind God, I just found one." Yes, it is easy not to credit our gifts. Live with an attitude of gratitude and see if it is not true that more good funnels your way.

Have you ever noticed that when you start your day off poorly it seems to continue or even get worse? That is because we tend to get more of what we focus on. This is a key lesson to learn. You wake up late and as you hurry out of bed you stub your toe into your dresser. You scream and hobble over to the shower. Thinking about your toe, you turn the shower on without paying attention only to step into scalding hot water. And, so goes the continuation of a long and dreadful day. You are laser focused on only your problems, thus causing more problems. The answer, once again, is an attitude of gratitude. Then next time you wake up late, be grateful that you woke up at all. If you should happen to stub your toe, be grateful you have a toe or a foot for that matter. "I once was distraught because I had no shoes, until I met a man who had no feet." It won't be long until your positive attitude breaks your negative cycle. It takes practice but it will change your life and allow you much greater productivity towards fulfilling your mission.

One of the most powerful journals you can have is a Gratitude Journal. Write down all the things, the stories, and the people that you are grateful for. Add to it and reread it regularly. Consume yourself with gratitude and people and good things will be drawn your way. You're on your way to fulfilling your mission.

ATTITUDE OF HUNGER

Years ago, I asked Dan Williams, my earlier referenced business mentor, "What is the No. 1 quality you look for in an individual before you agree to mentor him?" He said simply, "Hunger." Then he explained, "I can teach a hungry person how to be sharp, but it is much more difficult to teach a sharp person how to be hungry." It is one thing to have your head involved; it is another to have also captured your heart. Hence, the saying, "When the student is ready, the teacher will appear." Resources arrive when you have a hungry attitude.

Your hunger will cause you to care less about what everyone else thinks and more about what it is that you are accomplishing.

Often, people find themselves in life doing something that they just don't have their heart in. They have head knowledge, but not heart hunger. Consequently, not only do they not feel satisfaction from what they do, they also know that they are not giving their best performance. However, when you are pursuing your purpose you will feel it. You will be hungry to

When you are pursuing your purpose you will feel it. You will be hungry to learn more, to do more and be more.

learn more, to do more and be more. You will be energized! You will be excited! Your hunger will cause you to care less about what everyone else thinks and more about what it is that you are accomplishing.

There is a story of a young boy fishing with his grandfather. The two would sit together for hours in their small row boat talking and fishing. The grandfather had many stories and life experiences to share and had become very successful over the course of his life. One day while casting his line out again, the young boy asked his grandfather what was the secret to his success. Almost instantly, the grandfather knocked the boy on the back, causing him to fall into the water. Just as the boy grabbed the boat to begin to pull himself up, the grandfather pushed the boy's head underwater and held it there! After what seemed like forever, he let the boy's head up. The boy gasped for air only to feel his grandfather push his head back under water again! This process repeated several times until finally the boy began thrashing about in the water trying desperately to break free. The grandfather released him and pulled him back into the boat. The boy, coughing and still gasping for air, blurted out, "Why did you do that?!" The grandfather calmly responded, "When you want to succeed as much as you wanted air, you'll have it. Your success in anything is directly related to the level of hunger you have for it."

> *Your success in anything is directly related to the level of hunger you have for it.*

In the late 1990s, I traveled to Eastern Europe for a series of speaking engagements in Poland and the Czech Republic. I fell in love with the people there as they are truly some of the warmest people I have ever met. They also are some of the hungriest people. I will never forget my experience at the end of an event in Prague in front of approximately 12,000 people.

The event was coming to a close and I, along with all the other speakers, was standing on the stage for the concluding remarks and a video presentation. The arena went dark and, on the JumboTron screens, a film clip began of the Warner Bros. movie, "Free Willy." I had seen the movie and recognized the final scene that was being shown. It was where Willy, a killer whale, was in a lagoon area preparing to jump over a land barrier to its freedom in the ocean. There was a little boy on his hands and knees encouraging Willy to go for it quickly before Willy's captors arrived. Willy began circling, preparing for his jump. Then, all of a sudden, all 12,000 people in the arena stood up and started pounding their feet on the metal stadium floor. They also started chanting something in Czech. The noise was thundering! It seemed that the entire arena was shaking. I was looking around, my head and ears were pounding. I remember thinking, "I think this place is about to crash down!" I leaned over to my interpreter who was standing next to me and asked what everyone was chanting. I didn't get a response. I looked closer and realized in the darkness that my interpreter couldn't speak as tears were streaming down his face. I asked again, "What is everyone saying?" He looked over at me in a barely audible volume and a quivering voice and said, "Freedom. They are chanting freedom!" Just then, Willy made the jump over the barrier and made it into the ocean. And, instantly the place erupted at an even higher volume with screaming, pounding, clapping, whistling. It kept going on and on. My ears rang. The arena shook. Then, it hit me. Every one of these 12,000 people understood what it felt like to gain their freedom. Less than 10 years earlier, every one of them lived behind the constraints of the Iron Curtain. They knew what it felt like not to be able to pursue their dreams. They knew what it felt like to be under the rule of another. To them, "Free Willy" wasn't a cute children's movie. To them, "Free Willy" was their story. No wonder the arena was completely filled for the weekend to hear our talks on Free Enterprise. No wonder people were willing to literally ride their bicycles to get there as many didn't have a car. No wonder they were so hungry! They understood better than most the incredible value of truly being able to freely enterprise and achieve dreams.

ATTITUDE OF POSSIBILITY THINKING

You can focus on the fact that it probably won't happen for you or you can focus on the possibility that it will. Many Christians have a common favorite verse, "I can do all things though Christ who strengthens me." (Philippians 4:13) I may not be able to do it on my own but with God I can do it. That's powerful. Do you believe it? If so, does your attitude show it? With the God of the universe on your side, how could you possibly say that it is not possible?! Now, that's bold! I find myself constantly asking God for his assistance then, rightfully, giving him full credit for the victory.

This type of faith-based, possibility living doesn't give permission to deny all common sense and claim any activity is possible under the heading of "being positive." If you walk out onto a narrow train track and stand waiting for a train to pass through, proclaiming you have faith that you won't be hurt, that really isn't "being positive." More accurately, it's "being stupid." There are things called "common sense" and "cause and effect" and a multi-ton train smashing into your body at 65 mph tends to have a very predictable rearranging effect on your body. What I'm talking about here is living faith-based such that just because the odds in life don't look good from your vantage point, you still choose to believe everything is possible. To quote one of America's modern-day philosophers, Jim Carrey, let me recap a scene from the brilliant movie, "Dumb & Dumber." Carrey was told by the girl of his dreams that the odds were one-in-a-million of them ever getting together. To that, he responded, "So...you're telling me there's a chance!" OK, maybe I'm stretching it a bit, but you get the point.

Constantly ask, "What is possible?" or "How can I?" Many people spend all their energy convincing themselves and everyone around them that they "can't" do something. In many cases,

> *Constantly ask, "What is possible?" or "How can I?"*

if a fraction of that energy was simply put towards saying, "How can I?" then amazing things would result. Have you ever found yourself saying, "I can't afford it," or "I don't have the time"? Well, you're right. You have already limited yourself by determining that it's a fact. Consequently, you will experience that you don't have the money or the time which will then reinforce your negative attitude. Consequently, the next time you will be even more confident that you don't have the money or the time as you recall your last experience. It's a negative, self-fulfilling prophecy. However, imagine instead if you asked, "How can I afford it?" or "How can I find the time?" Just as you ask those questions, can't you feel your mental wheels shift gears and begin turning forward? How can I...? The subconscious mind goes to work on a solution. The mental gates are open to receive inspiration. The awareness factor skyrockets regarding anything that may play a role in the ability to make it happen. In other words, the right question alone dramatically increases your possibility of success. When this process does lead to a positive solution, you begin building a positive expectation. "The impossible is really possible" becomes an established belief and the basis of a positive, self-fulfilling prophecy.

The point is to leave the land of impossibility, start with possibility and grow to expectation. People don't generally get what they want, they get what they expect. And, the ultimate form of expectancy is when you believe it is God's will. "Thy will be done..." says the Lord's Prayer. If it is His will, then certainly a door will open if you are asking and looking for it.

One of the greatest examples of possibility thinking goes back to 1961 and U.S. President John F. Kennedy. On May 25, 1961, President Kennedy announced before a special joint session of Congress the dramatic and ambitious goal of sending an American safely to the moon and back before the end of the decade. He said, "First, I believe that this nation should commit itself to achieving the goal, before this decade is out, of landing a man on the moon and returning him safely to the earth. No single space project in this period will be more impressive to mankind, or more important for the long-range exploration of space; and none will be so difficult or expensive to accomplish." The technology needed had yet to be invented. To many people around the world, it was an absolute impossibility. Yet, eight years later on July 20, 1969, it was accomplished. It was estimated that approximately 500 million people around the world listened and watched the event as Neil Armstrong announced, "Houston, Tranquility Base here. The Eagle has landed." Then, six hours later, Armstrong descended the ladder, stepped off, paused a moment, and stated the immortal line, "That's one small step for [a] man, one giant leap for mankind." The impossible happened. Plus, he shot one under par!

There are times when we really must work hard not to let our own self-imposed limitations dictate what can and cannot be done. Often, we don't even know that we do it. We simply notice the bar of achievement that others have reached and subconsciously limit ourselves to that point. There are fantastic stories of people accomplishing greatness when they were simply unaware of where the bar of achievement was set. One of the best examples of unknowingly raising the bar is a story about George Dantzig.

In Dantzig's own words, "During my first year at Berkeley I arrived late one day to one of [Dr. Jerzy] Neyman's classes. On the blackboard were two problems which I assumed had been assigned for homework. I copied them down. A few days later I apologized to Neyman for taking so long to do the homework — the problems seemed to be a little harder to do than usual. I asked him if he still wanted the work. He told me to throw it on his desk. I did so reluctantly because his desk was covered with such a heap of papers that I feared my homework would be lost there forever. About six weeks later, one Sunday morning about eight o'clock, Anne and I were awakened by someone banging on our front door. It was Neyman. He rushed in with papers in hand, all excited: "I've just written an introduction to one of your papers. Read it so I can send it out right away for publication." For a minute I had no idea what he was talking about. To make a long story short, the problems on the blackboard which I had solved thinking they were homework were in fact two famous unsolved problems in statistics. That was the first inkling I had that there was anything special about them."

George Dantzig unknowingly solved statistical problems that up until that day had been unsolvable. However, by being under the context of thinking it was a homework assignment, Dantzig had the advantage of total possibility thinking on his side. He not only thought it had already been done but assumed that the entire class was solving them also. He didn't limit himself and continued to search for an answer until he ultimately figured it out.

The key is not only having an attitude of possibility thinking once in a while, but making it a regular thought process in your life. You may not be sending a man to the moon or solving an unsolvable statistics problem, but just as important is accomplishing the many impossibilities that come your way day to day.

My Grandmother Elizabeth (the sister of my Great Uncle George) was one of the sweetest people to ever walk the face of the earth. She was 97 years old when she was visiting my parents and me in Orange County, Calif. She had a remarkable life, being married to my Grandfather Roy for 73 years before he passed. She told stories of living in Chicago with the "young man" who was such a "terrible troublemaker," referring to Al Capone. She would recap hearing the news as a young girl of the sinking of the Titanic while my Grandfather Roy shared his experience meeting old Civil War veterans that visited his school as a child. Her life had been very full and she told us that her only remaining wish was to pass peacefully in her home like her husband had and not in a hospital. That is all she wanted as a final wish.

During this particular trip, she had a devastating stroke. She was raced to the hospital but, unfortunately, her condition continued to deteriorate. She was fighting pneumonia in a near comatose state, only making periodic moans but without any real communication.

I remember watching my dad talk with the doctor. My dad

asked how can we get her home — she lived near Salinas, Calif., about a six-hour drive north of the hospital. The doctor's response was direct: "You can't."

"No," my dad responded. "How can we?"

"You can't," repeated the doctor. "She won't make the trip — she's too weak. Besides, I have no ability to schedule an ambulance to take her that far for no reason."

"But there must be a way to get her there. How is it possible?" my dad persisted.

"The only way I can think of is if you personally hire a medical transport aircraft and fly her there," the doctor said, finally responding to my dad's possibility questioning. "But, that would make no sense. It would be tremendously expensive and it won't make a difference to her."

"It will make all the difference in the world," my dad said. "It is her final wish."

Only hours later, I remember the tears rolling down my face as I watched my dad wheeling his mom on a stretcher across the tarmac to the waiting medical transport plane. The sun was just setting and rays of golden light beamed through my grandma's silver hair that was flowing in the wind. "You're heading home, mom. I'm taking you home," I could hear my dad softly saying to her. The plane landed and an ambulance took her with a medical crew to her home. There, her family including her son and daughter-in-law, her granddaughter, and all her great-great grandchildren gathered around her bed to say goodbye. Amazingly, her moaning stopped completely. She had a very peaceful look on her face. I knew it had made a difference. Possibility thinking and my dad asking, "How can we?" gave a beautiful lady her final wish.

Create the habit of being a possibility thinker. Realize that although you originally are told or even believe that "you can't," if you just start asking, "How can I?" you open the door to miracles. God isn't glorified when you can do it without Him. Consequently, making possible from the impossible is His business. In the process of pursuing His purpose for your life, this is a necessity.

CHAPTER 18

Actions

The road to failure is paved with good intentions.
Actions, not intentions, make progress.
—Anonymous

BELIEF SYSTEM ➤ EMOTIONS ➤ ATTITUDE ➤ **ACTIONS** ➤ RESULTS

Up to this point, everything has been about your thoughts. Your core values led to your Beliefs. Your Beliefs trigger your emotions and corresponding attitude. Your attitude directs your actions. This is the bridge from the internal to the external. As quoted earlier, Ralph Waldo Emerson said, "The ancestor to every action is a thought." Our thinking precedes our actions —even if, for some, it is just a little bit.

> *Once you have created your Life Purpose Statement, continually ask yourself if an activity is moving you toward your Mission in life to fulfill your Life Purpose? Are you "Supporting yourself?"*

Once you have created your Life Purpose Statement, continually ask yourself if an activity is moving you toward your Mission in life to fulfill your Life Purpose. Are you "Supporting yourself?" This concept may be totally new for you if you never had a Life Purpose Statement before. However, you'll be amazed at how things will have a different meaning to you now that you and not Simon have clarified a vision for your life. Focus your energy on activities that move you towards your vision. Author Brian Tracy said, "You can tell how important something is today by measuring its potential future impact on your life." Be willing to sacrifice short-term for the long-term benefits that fulfill your Life Mission. As Peter Drucker said, "Efficiency is doing things right, but effectiveness is doing the right things."

> *"You can tell how important something is today by measuring its potential future impact on your life."*
> —*Brian Tracy*

ESTABLISHING PRIORITIES

Where do you begin taking action? Always begin with the end in mind. The end objective is now clear: True your Wheel of Life and fulfill your Life Purpose. That is, the objective is to expand and balance your Wheel of Life by applying your purpose to each domain of it, live by your core values and go after your calling, your assignment.

Through this focus, your life will be expanding! Of course, some domains will be expanding faster than others so life will never be in perfect balance. However, given your desire for balance and awareness of it, you will never have to experience the dangerous sudden realization of some extreme imbalance. Your life is not happening by chance. It is not an accident. You are living on purpose.

Let's get it going and take action now! Referring back to your Wheel of Life, review each domain and picture each of them as they are in your life. Next, imagine what each domain would look like in your life as it became ideal. Transfer this vision onto a separate piece of paper for each domain by simply writing a list of wants that made the difference. Some domains will have more wants than others. Please do not read on without taking a moment to write down a vision and wants for each of the eight domains of your life. This is your one and only precious life...take a moment to seriously cast a written vision for where you are going.

Once you complete this, it's time to have a **Priorities Tournament.** A Priorities Tournament is a game played to determine what wants have priority over others. Without this game, the list you just created may look overwhelming and, consequently, be depressing. That would not be good nor very helpful during the pursuit of an on-purpose life. Fortunately, this process will immediately eliminate any such feelings by easily recognizing which wants win and takes the top spot in the priority list.

There are essentially two tournaments: The qualifying rounds and the Finals. In the qualifying rounds, place each of the wants of a particular domain onto the far left lines of the grid below. Then, let the playoffs begin. Ask yourself, if I had to choose between the first and the second want, which one would I choose? Game, set, match. Advance the winner to the next line to the right. Do that for all the wants of the domain, eliminating half of them. Then, repeat the process with the next column of wants and repeat until you ultimately end with the final winner.

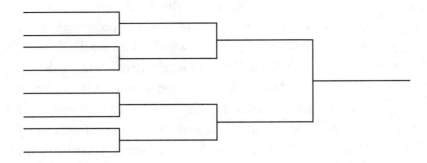

When you have completed this process for each of the eight domains of your life, this completes the qualifying round. You now have the top priority of each area of your life. Looking at your Life Purpose Statement, are each of them in alignment? Are they in line with your core values and Personal Mission Statement? If not, modify it or disqualify it and replace it with a new winner. Also, make a mental note of how your purpose could be applied to make each happen, as well as how each directly or indirectly applies to your Personal Assignment.

With the final eight wants (the top pick of each domain), let the finals begin. Again, line these wants up in the first column of the grid and begin the playoffs. You are now choosing between wants of different domains but the process is the same. If you had to choose between the first and the second, which one would you choose? Again continue until you end with overall winner. Once completed, you now have the No. 1 priority picked in your life!

This information is tremendously helpful as you now have order and clarity of your wants and a prioritized list to make happen. Beginning with your overall priority, use the goal system to set into motion the process of turning your want into a reality. Travel down the list setting goals in order of priority. Set as many goals as you are comfortable with. Be careful of doing too much too soon. If this is your first day in the goal setting gym of life, take it easy. Grab a 5-lb. barbell. We want you back again tomorrow. In such a case, you may want to simply start with an action step for your top eight and work towards establishing goals. The key is to start taking action of some kind and begin the process of a living an on-purpose life!

Although during life you will certainly find yourself in activities that draw you off purpose, you will now have a much greater awareness of it. Getting back to on-purpose activities will become more and more natural and significantly more rewarding. Regularly review your Life Wheel and run tournaments anytime you are looking for renewed order and clarity in the pursuit of your Life Purpose.

As you move from the macro picture of your priorities down to the "roll up your sleeves and get to work" micro picture, you will want to confidently choose the right activities. A method to manage the best use of your time is taught by Steven Covey in his book, "The Seven Habits of Highly Effective People." In his book, Covey writes about recognizing the difference between items that are "Urgent" vs. "Important". He explains that all of our activities fall into one of four areas: Important & Urgent, Important & Not Urgent, Not Important & Urgent, and Not Important & Not Urgent.

	Urgent (Simon Says)	Not Urgent
Important	Quadrant I	Quadrant II
Not Important	Quadrant III	Quadrant IV

Have you ever noticed that the important things in life "rarely ring" while the urgent almost always do? It is essential that we direct ourselves out of the non-important quadrants and back into the important quadrants. Beware of "Urgent" distractions. For example, you are doing something important when the phone rings. What do you do? Most of us instinctually run to answer the phone. Why? Is it really that important or did it ring and suddenly capture our attention? Covey says that most people will naturally do the items that are Urgent (Simon Says) and Important and not the non-Urgent and non-Important items. However, he says that the trick is to stay focused on completing items that are Important and non-Urgent (Quadrant II) over the items that are Urgent and non-Important (Quadrant III).

> *Stay focused on completing items that are Important and non-Urgent over the items that are Urgent and non-Important.*

A simple way to stay on track with this concept is to continually say, "WIN." WIN stands for the question, "What's Important Now?" In order to WIN in life, stay focused on doing the important rather than the urgent things. The most common explanation people share with me as to why they haven't achieved more is that they were "distracted" by life's drama. That is, people fail to keep the main thing the main thing (was that redundant?) amidst the many urgent distractions of life. Keep focused on doing What's Important Now and enjoy the rewards that come from it.

Another method of prioritizing your activities is using the A-E method. This is a simple method of writing everything down that needs to be done and assigning an A-E to them:

A – Item is **A**bsolutely necessary. It is very important and there are big consequences if it is not completed.
B – Item is **B**ig in importance but the consequences are not too severe if not completed.
C – Item has no **C**onsequences if not completed.
D – Item can be **D**elegated.
E – Item can be **E**liminated.

Remember, it's not about how much time you spend on tasks, but rather it's about how much time you spend on High-Priority tasks. Be sure to put as much time in as possible to the "A" and "B" tasks.

GOALS

Too often people are just responding to whatever life throws their way; basically always playing defense. It's an easy trap to fall into given all that comes at us in life. However, constantly playing defense is not the best strategy to make ground on fulfilling our Life Purpose. We must become proactive, set goals and take action. Effective goals, at a minimum, are specific and measurable. For example, saying, "I'm going to get into shape" doesn't work. Round and pear are shapes. Are either of those your goal? Yes, specific and measurable are keys. When you set a goal to achieve something specific, it is now time to implement a Pattern for Success.

The three most common approaches that people take toward achieving goals are the following: First, there is the "Ready, Fire, Aim," approach. These people just start firing before they have really prepared or planned at all. Who knows what's going to happen! Next, there is the "Ready, Aim, Aim, Aim" approach. These people are in the opposite camp. They are endlessly planning or preparing and never get to firing. Nothing ever actually happens. Finally, there is the "Ready, Aim, Fire," approach. This final group of people consider it, prepare and plan for it, and take action! The following is a very common-sense but powerful formula to implement this approach to any activity. In fact, it is so straightforward that many people will naturally discount it, looking for something more complex or sophisticated. There are many formulas for success but, if you really take a close look at them, ultimately they will boil down to this system.

Five-Step System for Success:
1. "Ready"--Assess the Situation
2. "Aim"--Plan and Prepare
3. "Fire"--Take Action
4. Review--Review the Results
5. Repeat--Repeat the Process

1. "Ready" — Assess the Situation

Before you take action, it is essential that you assess the situation. Remember the dialog with the border guard when I was at the border of United States and Canada? Most importantly, he asked where I was coming from, he clarified where I was, and he asked where I was going. Assessing any situation must include these three points.

First, before taking any action, it is wise to consider where you are coming from. That is, what are your core values and operating principles? Are they yours or Simon's?

Understanding where you are coming from allows you to see if where you are going will cause any misalignment. Will I be in conflict with my values or operating principles? If so, then there is no need to proceed. No success is more important than you successfully staying true to yourself. A core belief to lock into your belief system is, "There is no amount of happiness that results from success achieved while acting in opposition to my values and principles that can overcome the discomfort the misalignment develops simultaneously." This truth is so important.

> *There is no amount of happiness that results from success achieved while acting in opposition to your values and principles that can overcome the discomfort the misalignment develops simultaneously.*

It is easy to be romanced by the proposition of success and its many benefits. However, ultimately your greatest rewards include self-respect and the fulfillment of your Life Mission. Trust that if you must be compromised, then either another way will present itself or it just isn't as important as you have convinced yourself. This is a time you must be careful of your feelings; it may be time for a group hug. Often, the excitement of success can build to a point that it can encourage an extra level of rationalization as to why such a compromise of values or principles is really acceptable. It's not. Remember, "Rationalize" simply stands for, "Rational Lies."

> *Remember, "Rationalize" simply stands for, "Rational Lies."*

Once you've taken a clear look at your values and principles and everything is in alignment, then it is time to consider the border guard's clarification of where I was and his ensuing question of where I was going. That is, honestly assess: 1-Where are you currently? 2-A vision of where you want to be. Finally, define the gap between where you are and where you want to be. For example, if you are attempting to lose weight, you may assess where you are at by checking how much you currently weigh, what your eating and exercise habits look like, etc. Then, you would describe the vision you have: How much you weigh, what you look and feel like, as well as how you eat and exercise, etc. Finally, you complete the assessment by determining the existing gap between the two; your weight difference, eating and exercising differences, etc.

CURRENT ➤ GAP ➤ VISION

It is not only important to assess the reality of your current situation and the gap that exists, but also it is necessary to accept it. Without accepting this reality, it will be difficult to develop a plan that has any real odds of success. More likely you will set unreasonable goals and quickly become discouraged. Accepting the reality of your situation may be humbling, but remember, it doesn't matter where you are; it only matters where you are going.

2. "Aim" — Plan and Focus

PLAN

Based on your Assessment, develop a supportive game plan to bridge your gap. This is the step many people skip in their excitement to act. Action is good, but directed action gets results. If the results are worth pursuing then they are worth planning. To develop an effective and complete plan, answer the following five questions:

1-Why is it important to you?
2-When is it going to happen?
3-What are the most important actions to take?
4-How are you going to increase your knowledge on the topic?
5-Who is going to support it?

1-(Your Energy): Why is it important to you? Every game plan must have a reason. There is simply no point to proceed beyond this step if you don't have a good answer since you won't have your heart in it. However, with a clear understanding as to why it is important to you, you now have the motivation — the reason — to follow-through and succeed. Once you answer this question, again ask, "Why is that important?" Keep asking "Why?" until you have gotten down to the emotion and belief that is behind your motivation. Not only will it get you in touch with the deeper passion to really move you forward, but it also allows you to check your belief behind your motivation to see that it is truly aligned with your core values and not Simon's. For example, let's suppose you want to earn more money to buy a new car. That's fine but why is it important? "Because it is a cool car," you say. Yes, it is — but why is that important? "Because I'd feel successful driving it." Why is that important? "Because if I were successful, I'd be admired." It would appear based on this quick inspection that admiration may well be a core value and you believe that success yields admiration. Is it a core value or is something else leading you to currently desire admiration? In addition, is "success yields admiration" a solid, accurate and healthy belief? Asking these deeper questions will clarify the substance of your motivation.

Given alignment between your core values and the beliefs behind your motivation, you now have discovered a deep, worthy motivation. With this clarity, you can also easily look for additional ways to achieve it. If they are not in alignment, then this pursuit won't lead to deep satisfaction. In which case, the motivation, and its supportive belief, may well deserve some closer consideration before applying it. This process may seem unnecessary or tedious, but it is really valuable and over time it becomes very simple.

> *Understand that a clearly defined worthy passion is the most important ingredient of your success strategy.*

Understand that a clearly defined worthy passion is the most important ingredient of your success strategy. It will be called upon regularly during the action phase and it will drive you to your best performance.

Recently, I competed in the U.S. Ultra-Running Nationals in the 24-hour competition. If you ever want to learn about yourself, I recommend running for 24 hours straight. Well, on second thought, it might not be my first recommendation but you would certainly have the opportunity to get well acquainted with yourself during such an event. Your body and mind will both be communicating with you at a volume that you definitely can't miss. During my adventures of running in 24-hour competitions, I have learned a lot about myself; what keeps me going, what holds me back, what is important and what is not. Many of these discoveries can be applied in all areas of life and the most critical lesson of all is: Know Why!

I can teach you how to fuel your body during an extreme running event —how many grams of carbohydrates per hour, how many milligrams of sodium per hour, how much water, etc. However, if you can't answer the question of why you would do it, my information to you will simply become "knowledge on ice." It doesn't have value to you because you don't have a reason to use it — it doesn't support a burning passion.

Unfortunately, the recent Nationals was not my best race. The first 30 miles were good but it wasn't coming together well after that point. It's one thing to have a tough race and know that it will be over in a few minutes. It's another thing to know that you have nearly 20 hours to go! Regardless, it gave me an extra opportunity to get a better understanding of myself. There is always a good side. At hour 23, the course is shortened to a simple ¼-mile loop. My legs were fried after some 110+ miles of difficult racing. My body was way under-fueled. Blood was coming through my right shoe due to a sloppy shoe change some 12 hours earlier; fortunately, it had gone numb by this point. Sadly, my "why" had also gone numb as well as the best answer to "Why am I doing this?" was simply "to finish." That is barely a "why" at all and it clearly showed.

Everything changed instantly, however, when the race director announced over the PA system that Connie Gardner was on pace to set the women's American record! A new American record — I got inspired. Once I understood the great race that Connie was having, I got involved with her "why." "This is about making history...I must do all that I can to help her do it!" My "why" suddenly had great significance — to help someone make history! The combination of having a "why" of great significance as well as serving another person sent me on an internal mission to dig deep for energy. I put everything I had into moving faster...I focused everything on getting it going to encourage her. I was cheering for her while running. I found myself going faster and faster as my inspiration grew. It had to be one of the greatest lessons to me of the power of knowing "why" you are doing something and how you can achieve so much more than you ever thought possible when the "why" is significant enough.

Make a commitment to not only grow your knowledge of how to do things, but also to clarify your understanding of why you and not Simon are doing them. Then, like a boomerang, keep coming back to your why. Even when you are "on purpose," you can get so caught up with the "how to" that you lose touch with the inspiration that the "why to" provides. By doing this, watch your energy, productivity and fulfillment skyrocket both in the pursuit of your goals and in overall your life.

> *A goal is a vision with a date on it.*

2-(Your Timeline): When is it going to happen? A goal is a vision with a date on it. That is, if you say I want to achieve XYZ, but don't say by when, then you don't really have a goal; you still only have the vision. Set a completion goal date and set intermediate steps to be achieved every 30 days.

3-(Your Activity): What are the most important actions steps to take? It is easy to do what grabs your attention first, what seems urgent, or simply what you enjoy or have a habit doing. However, an effective plan includes determining the most important activities you can start doing that will contribute toward the realization of your vision as well as the items to stop doing that are holding you back. Create a new daily routine with this modification. Success is hidden in your daily routine!

4-(Your Knowledge): How are you going to increase your knowledge on the topic? We have all heard the phrase, "Don't just work hard, work smart." However, you can't apply what you don't know so constantly seek more knowledge. Einstein said, "We cannot solve our problems with the same thinking we used to create them." Applied knowledge is power to succeed. What can you do to increase your knowledge? Put learning into your daily routine through reading, listening to educational programs, attending seminars, and receiving coaching/mentoring from qualified individuals. Education is an investment but it is the best investment you can make for yourself. And, remember, if you think education is expensive, try ignorance. In life, either you will learn from someone else's experience or you will learn from your own. In business, there is a saying, "When a man with money meets a man with experience, the man with experience ends up with the money and the man with the money ends up with an experience." There is always more to know about your vision. And, after you ripen, you rot so stay hungry to grow in knowledge.

> *If you think education is expensive, try ignorance. In life, either you will learn from someone else's experience or you will learn from your own.*

5-(Your Team): Who is going to support it? I have yet to meet a "self-made man/woman." In every case, there are always others who played a key role in their success. Who is going to be a part of your "success team?" Specifically, create a success team that includes: those you can count on for support, those you can be accountable to, and those who can coach you. Everyone, and I mean everyone, needs support. Who can you look to simply for support? Seek out people to comprise that team. Next, consider who you can be accountable to. Let's face it, when you are accountable to someone, the pressure is on. It is a lot easier to fall short when nobody else knows it. However, when you have an accountability person or team you will find you naturally put out that extra effort. Finally, who is going to coach you? Even the very best have coaches. Find someone with knowledge and successful experience who is willing to coach you.

FOCUS

While descending down the Santa Barbara, Calif. mountainside, I quickly glance down at the digital speedometer on my road bike...40, 45, 50 mph it was reading. "Stay on my wheel!" my riding buddy yells to me as we continue our insanely fast descent down the mountain. "Press down — outer foot!" his coaching continues. Every fiber of my being is focusing on this moment. "Hang with him!" I tell myself. "I can do this!" I confess. "I better or I'm dead!" another voice goes off in my head. "Shut up!" I tell it. "I'm gonna die..." it repeats. "Great job!" my riding buddy yells, interrupting my internal argument. "Stay with him" I go back to telling myself.

Years ago, I was racing triathlons and a cyclist friend of mine was helping me dramatically improve my riding (and in this case my descending) techniques. Learning to corner downhill comes with practice and, for me, a significant amount of focus. I had crashed in numerous rides with the road-rash scars and destroyed equipment to prove it. It was time to get some coaching. I found myself crashing even while following my coach but each time I did he would remind me that it was for the same reason. Focus.

Without proper focus the plan is pointless. We are either properly focused, focused on the wrong thing or not focused at all. The key is to focus on the right thing at the right time.

Author Mike Murdoch says, "The only reason men fail is broken focus." Distractions can cause serious harm (crashes) during a cycling race but they can cause serious harm to the fulfillment of one's goals in life as well. In our daily life, I have found that often the task at hand isn't actually all that difficult but it's staying focused that can take most of the effort. Most of us have so many things happening in our life it tends to be difficult to stay focused on any one thing. We find ourselves "putting out fires" all the time — handling this and that — and it keeps us from ever really staying on target. Add in massive amounts of media hitting us constantly from every direction and, finally, often our greatest distraction of all — the cell phone. Why is it that no matter what we are doing, if our phone rings we have this huge need to answer it? We could be in the middle of a complex situation or even enjoying a quiet, intimate moment, but if the phone rings, watch out! I've seen people hear their phone and literally propel themselves across the room in order to reach it in time without even knowing who may be calling. "I'm sorry, looks like you have the wrong number." It's fascinating, really.

I watched a couple eat dinner the other night each on their cell phones most of the time. It took me back to a saying my dad repeated often as I grew up, "Wherever you are, be there." If you are with someone, be there. If you are doing something, do it. Have you ever been at work thinking about what is happening back home or at home thinking about what you need to be doing at work? In this case, you are being distracted by your own thoughts. Be wherever you are — be present in the present.

A final distraction that needs some recognition in this discussion is the ever-so disguised distraction often referred to as "Opportunity." Opportunities are just that — an opportunity for potential success or an opportunity to be distracted from your current focus. Regardless of whether the distraction was external as from a phone call, an internal thought, or a disguised one as an opportunity, the result is the same: you crashed because of your broken focus.

There are numerous books on maintaining focus but most will incorporate some combination of setting short-term, realistic goals, along with having an accountability program in place. The short-term goals should be simple to achieve and when put together are in line with the overall, long-term goal. The accountability program is the simple idea of having someone else that you are going to be accountable to at the end of the day. It is interesting but true that most of us will do more to avoid letting someone down that we respect than we even will do for ourselves. Finally, staying focused is also a great deal more likely when a very clear and meaningful reward and consequence are in place for its completion or lack of completion. Staying focused is a personal science. Learn as much as you can about it and discover what works best for you.

Focused on the wrong thing...Nearly every crash on my bike was a two step process: Step 1-Loose focus, Step 2-Regain focus on where I didn't want to go. This was not a good combination. The idea isn't to be focused on where you don't want to go but rather where you do want to go. "The last thing you ever want to do on these descents down the mountain is to look over the cliff," my cycling coach would say. "Wherever your eyes go, your bike and body will follow." Similarly, wherever your focus goes, so will be your life. As the Bible says, "As a man thinketh, so is he."

Unfortunately, in life just as in cycling, the negative that comes at us quickly — whether in the form of a cliff we are flying towards at 50 mph or an ever-increasing credit card debt — tends to grab our attention. Our desire to avoid pain often causes us to focus on that which has the ability to cause it. The more we allow it to grab our attention, the more we focus on it, the more we begin to gravitate to it or it to us. Have you ever noticed how the bad can get worse? You find yourself in a negative spiral downward. Let's say that you are drowning in debt. It is such a heavy burden that it probably is on your mind all the time and the pressure is killing you. You keep saying, "I must get out of debt." The problem is that you are focused on the concept of "Debt." Even though you are saying you want to "get out" of debt the subject is still debt and it still feels draining. Consequently, although you want out, you will more likely end up in more debt as you move closer to the subject you are focused on. The solution is not to focus on "getting out of debt" but rather on "getting into financial abundance" (or some positive alternative).

Only focus on where you want to go. Strengthen your mind to be able to resist the temptation of looking at or thinking about where you don't want to go; not by not going there, but by focusing on a positive alternative. Replace the negative focus with an opposing positive one. It does take practice but your mind will get stronger. Entertaining the negative what-ifs can certainly be a natural and tempting activity but it doesn't lead to what you want to achieve. Consequently, put all your resources towards maintaining focus on your desired target.

> *Strengthen your mind to be able to resist the temptation of looking at or thinking about where you don't want to go; not by not going there, but by focusing on a positive alternative.*

Prior to actor Jim Carrey achieving big success, he wrote a check to himself in the amount of $10 million dollars for 'acting services rendered,' postdated Thanksgiving, 1995. When times were tough he would sit on a hill side of Los Angeles and imagine his coming success while re-reading his check. He kept the focus on where he wanted to go. Interestingly, a few years later, he signed a deal to act in a sequel to the movie The Mask for in excess of $10 million dollars. This agreement was done just prior to Thanksgiving, 1995. In his own words, "I wrote it (the check) as an affirmation of everything I've learned," he told Parade Magazine . "It wasn't about money. I knew if I was making that much, I'd be working with the best people on the best material. That's always been my dream. If you give up your dream, what's left?"

Keep focused on your desired victory. In 1970, sociologist Dr. Edward Banfield of Harvard University described a profound study on success and priority setting. He was searching for why some people became financially independent in their lifetime while others did not. He expected to find that financial success was primarily a result of various outside influences yet concluded that ultimately it came down to a personal mindset. He concluded that the most successful people had, what he termed, a "long time perspective." Today, the term we more commonly hear is "long-term perspective." The most successful people in life, financially or otherwise, were those who took the future into consideration with every decision they made in the present. It all comes down to what are you really looking to achieve when it is all said and done. Sure, having a third helping of cake at the party is enjoyable in the present, but when that sugar turns to fat is it really the result you wish to have long term? I know what you're thinking...well, it depends? What kind of cake is it?

In Daniel Goleman's pioneering book, "Emotional Intelligence," he discussed a study done with a group of 4-year-olds and marshmallows. They tested the children's EQs (Emotional Quotient – A term he coined) with the intent to determine whether it or IQ had a more profound effect on one's future success. In this study, the children were placed in a room individually at a table with two marshmallows. They were given the following proposal: If you wait until after he runs an errand, you can have two marshmallows for a treat. If you can't wait until then, you can only have one — but you can have it right now. The results were dramatic. When observing these same children as they were graduating high school, in Goldman's own words, "Those who resisted the temptation at 4 were now, as adolescents, more socially competent: personally effective, self-assertive, and better able to cope with the frustrations of life. They were less likely to go to pieces, freeze, or regress under stress, or become rattled or disorganized when pressured; they embraced challenges and pursued them instead of giving up even in the face of difficulties; they were self-reliant and confident, trustworthy and dependable; and they took initiative and plunged into projects. And, more than a decade later, they were still able to delay gratification in pursuit of their goals." The point is that one's success has much more to do with their EQ than their IQ. This should be great news because your IQ is fixed and never changes, however, your EQ can increase with personal development. Think about it; that should make sense. You may never be great at solving math problems but you can learn to walk away from that cake that you feel keeps calling your name.

It was just after the America's Civil War, a mother had the opportunity to ask Gen. Robert E Lee for advice about raising her son. She approached the general and asked him, "If you can share any words of wisdom with my son, what would it be?" Gen. Lee looked at the mother and said, "Teach him to deny himself." Simple, but extremely profound words. In today's world everything is instant or we are not interested. Microwaves beat out ovens most of the time and even then we stand in front of them waiting. Fast food dominates the restaurant industry. Dial-up what? Soon, most people will never know what the little hourglass was all about that came up on our computer screens. We want it fast and we want it now. Marketing tells us that we deserve everything immediately so charge it now and pay for it later. Unfortunately, for the play now and pay later Simon crowd, that's a formula for disaster.

Dr. Banfield, Dr. Goleman and Gen. Lee were right: our best interest will result when we are emotionally mature enough to deny ourselves in the present in order to do what is best for the long term. How do you know what is best for the long term? Your Life Purpose Statement is your guide. As mentioned earlier, continually ask yourself, "Is this activity in line with my core values and is it moving me toward fulfilling my mission in life? Am I "Supporting myself or Simon?" Be willing to sacrifice short-term for the long-term benefits that fulfill your Life Purpose. Staying focused on these long-term benefits yield strength in the present and is your best tool to stay the course. Author Steven Covey calls it, "Living with the end in mind."

3. "Fire" — Take Action

It's time to take Action!!! Nothing happens until eventually somebody does something. That somebody is you and your time is now. Be careful of staying in the "Aim" stage for too long or you may never get out of it; paralysis from analysis (ready, aim, aim, aim...). If you stare at something long enough, it tends to get blurry. Yes, it's time to "Fire!" Think about it...You don't wait for all the lights to turn green before you start a trip, do you? It's time to start rolling. Using your plan to direct you, let the fun begin!

> *Nothing happens until eventually somebody does something.*

The successful process of taking action on your goal should go through three phases:

- Start — Take action; get the ball rolling.
- Apply — Self-discipline to keep things rolling.
- Develop — Supportive habits for long-term success.

Start – Take action; get the ball rolling.

There are many reasons why we never even start something. However, fear is often the case. We fear failure. We fear looking stupid to other people. We sometimes even fear success and the responsibility it may require. We fear pain and the possibility of a past pain resulting again with a new start. We certainly fear the unknown as it may contain the manifestation of all of these fears. Sometimes it runs even deeper as we feel conflicted and don't know why. For example, we may have a belief that "Money is the root of all evil." We have an opportunity to make money but unconsciously we hesitate to start because, unknowingly, we don't want to bring "evil" into our life. When you find yourself hesitating, go back to that great question we asked a lot earlier: "Why?" Why am I feeling hesitant? What is holding me back from starting? Keep asking why until you get back to your root belief. How's that belief working for you? Is it time to update it? Taking action on a goal is a great way to uncover faulty beliefs as you identify your hesitations. It is also an opportunity to once again depend upon a foundation of faith and a dash of courage to start.

"Go get some results," my early financial mentor, Dan Williams, told me when I first began working with him. "I'll do my best," I responded.

"Oh" he said. "I didn't mean to go out and necessarily get positive results. I just meant any results at all. It's very hard to steer a parked car, you know? Even if you start driving in the wrong direction, it will be much easier to turn the wheel around once you're moving then if you were just sitting there."

Yes, it's easy to replay the past and, consequently, fear starting anything at all. But, it's time to pre-play the vision of the future with faith and an attitude of possibility thinking.

Another hesitation behind not starting is simply comfort.

Too often a person is simply too comfortable to go after it. Comfort is the enemy of excellence. It can often be the barrier between you and your potential.

There's an old story that took place in the hills of Tennessee. A man was sitting in his rocking chair on the porch

> *Comfort is the enemy of excellence.*

of his shanty out in the woods. A neighbor came by and, as he approached the man, an old hound dog lying on the porch lifted his head, let out a slow but somewhat long-lasting moan then put his head back down. The neighbor, noticing but saying nothing, began opening conversation with the man just as the old hound did the same thing again: lifting up his head, letting out that slow, almost painful-sounding moan and then putting his head back down. Looking at the dog now, the neighbor finally asked, "What's wrong with your dog?"

To which the man in the chair while still rocking said, "Ain't nothing wrong with the dog."

"Well, then why is he making such an awful-sounding moaning noise?"

"Oh that," the man responded, "That's because he's lying on a nail."

"What?! He's lying on a nail? Why doesn't he get up and move?" the neighbor asked.

"Well, it doesn't hurt enough to get up and move. It only hurts enough to lay there and complain about it."

We can become comfortable even with our discomfort. We may find it easier to complain about it than do something about it. This is a very dangerous place to be because we can fall into a lifestyle of "looking for listeners." As long as we have an audience, we'll keep talking. The "supportive" audience actually enables the continuation of the complaining, comfortable lifestyle. Sadly but true, too many people relate to the words of Pink Floyd's song, "Comfortably Numb," as David Gilmour sings, "The child is grown, the dream is gone. I have become comfortably numb."

Similarly, some people aren't complaining about their discomfort but rather are simply basking in their comfort. That is, they aren't lying on a nail but too comfortable to move; rather, they are truly just too comfortable to move. The challenge here isn't about being a complainer but rather having a severe case of selfishness. You are set, so why do anything else? Well, because life really isn't about you. It's not about you surviving or succeeding — it's about being "significant." It's about serving others and fulfilling your God-given Life Purpose. If this is you, I am happy for your comfort. I hope you are grateful for it. In fact, I hope you are grateful enough that you feel compelled to help others who aren't as comfortable as yourself.

Comfort is not to be confused with contentment. Contentment is a deep sense of peace that comes from a spiritual understanding of God's grace and all that it means to you. A person is content regardless of their degree of comfort. However, people with excessive comfort will often realize that they have yet to experience contentment.

Apply – Self-discipline to keep things rolling.

Self-discipline is the ability to get yourself to take action regardless of your emotional state. Consequently, your self-discipline needed to take action brings us right back to raising our Emotional Quotient (EQ). Your ability to be self-disciplined can increase just as can your muscular strength from working out. If you pump your muscles, they will become strong. If you don't, they will weaken and, eventually, atrophy. Your mind and its ability to be self-disciplined operate in much the same way. So, if you shudder at the concept of being self-disciplined, hang in there, help is on the way. With some knowledge on the subject, you will be amazed what you will be able to do. Most likely, you just had some bad experiences which created a belief that you are not a self-disciplined person and you have lived accordingly ever since. The truth is, if you went into the gym without any instruction, you may come out with a similar conclusion. Since you don't know what weights to lift, you grab whatever. What are the odds that you will either grab weights that are too heavy or too light? After a certain amount of frustration or possibly injury, you may well conclude that the weightlifting thing just isn't for you.

When I was training for the Nationals and the Olympic Games, my USA swimming coach, Mike Troy, used to say, "Remember, the practice you miss is the one your competitor doesn't." That phrase used to haunt me because I knew I was competing off of my training given I had very little talent for actually swimming. In fact, when I qualified for the Olympic Trials, I remember him saying, "You are the fastest swimmer with the least amount of talent that I have ever coached." I took the compliment side of that since the talent part was obvious. As a two-time gold medalist himself in the 1960 Rome Olympics, a former Navy Seal and Vietnam veteran, he taught me a lot about self-discipline.

One morning, all the swimmers showed up for practice and he wasn't at the pool. It was 5 a.m., dark and cold. There was a posted message on a board explaining that he couldn't be there and to do the workout posted. What followed was interesting. Some guys literally just turned around and went home. Some guys got in the water but messed around most of the time. A few of us actually worked out like any other day, following his posted instructions. Now don't get me wrong, I *wanted* to go home or mess around. It wasn't like I was some amazingly self-disciplined person, as I might have appeared. The truth was I knew if I wanted the gold medal I personally couldn't afford to miss practice.

That afternoon, Coach Troy called a team meeting before the beginning of our afternoon practice. He informed us that he had an interesting morning. He pointed to the restaurant above the pool and shared how this morning he enjoyed a good breakfast there. You could have heard a pin drop. "Yes, the breakfast was good but what I observed was disturbing," he said. I remember thinking that I had never before been so grateful to lack talent. He went on, "You guys are some of the best swimmers in the country but I'm not here to babysit you, I'm here to coach you. You must develop self-discipline."

> *Self-discipline is a combination of will-power and perseverance.*

Self-discipline is a combination of willpower and perseverance:

Willpower

Just as the general concept of self-discipline can cause a person to shudder a bit, the specific component of willpower can yield even greater reactions. That's because willpower is typically misunderstood. Most people feel they don't have much willpower because they expected too much from it.

Willpower is not a long-term strategy; it is not for the marathon but for the sprint. Willpower will almost always run out well before the goal is achieved — which, consequently, has given it a poor reputation. However, when you understand that willpower is a short, significant burst of discipline then you can better determine its best application. Willpower shouldn't be the plan mode of apparatus to achieve your goal but rather to attack the obstacles that are holding you back. For example, rather than relying on willpower to see you through a lengthy exercise program, let it be used to set up a new environment conducive to staying the course. Perhaps you find a photo of the results you wish to obtain, get a gym membership, commit to a workout class, and create an accountability program with a friend. Your obstacle is a lack of motivation that takes you off track from your workout program. Your willpower attacked this obstacle by clarifying your vision (through finding a photo of what the results may look like), creating a schedule (through committing to the class), making a financial commitment that you obviously don't want wasted (through paying for a gym membership), as well as setting an accountability program with a friend (no one wants to embarrass themselves with a friend). These items have now positioned you into a new environment which is much more conducive to success. Hence, your short-lived willpower will now have a long-term, positive effect.

Perseverance

Nothing in the world can take the place of Persistence. Talent will not; nothing is more common than unsuccessful men with talent. Genius will not; unrewarded genius is almost a proverb. Education will not; the world is full of educated derelicts. Persistence and determination alone are

omnipotent. The slogan "Press On" has solved and always
will solve the problems of the human race.
— Calvin Coolidge

Perseverance is the long-term strategy. Opposite to the short, powerful bursts that willpower provides, perseverance is steady persistence. It operates in spite of difficulties, obstacles or discouragement. Perseverance can be increased simply by clarifying your vision. It is a matter of gaining more clarity on "Why" you are doing something. A clear and impactful vision will compel you to take action. When you clearly know where you are going and why you are going there, the means to that end may change but the effort continues. In other words, mentally the goal is set in stone while the plans are in sand.

> *There are three sources of "Why" motivation that will fuel your perseverance: External, Internal and Eternal.*

There are three sources of "Why" motivation that will fuel your perseverance:

- External — External motivation is the carrot that you desire to achieve. It is the new house, the vacation, the college tuition. It is "head motivation" as it is something external that connects with your mind. It is the first level of motivation.

- Internal — Internal motivation is what happens inside of you. It is the desire to earn respect, to stand for principle or something that stirs you internally. It is either "Heart motivation" when the internal desire comes from your heart or it is "Ego Motivation" when the internal desire comes from your ego. Heartfelt internal motivation is wonderful and is rooted in love. Ego-driven motivation, such as pride-based motivation, is dangerous with many undesirable side-effects.

Although both are powerful motivators, regularly assess from which type of internal motivation you are operating. Internal motivation is the second level of motivation.

• Eternal — Eternal motivation is what comes from making a difference with an eternal perspective in mind. It is something that will make a difference not just in your lifetime but beyond. As a result, it is much easier to endure and persist when you are doing something that can have eternal value. Motivation from God's will is "Spirit motivation" or being "In-spirit" or "Inspired" as it connects with your spirit. It is the third and highest level of motivation.

In addition to clarifying your vision and not Simon's, the next step to increased perseverance is accepting that fact that hard work is a part of the process. Whether the actual work itself is hard or easy at any given moment is irrelevant. It all needs to be done; the hard stuff and the easy, time-consuming stuff. It's about "paying your dues." Marketing companies know it best — appeal to our desire for results without hard work, "Perfect abdominal muscles in just three minutes of pain-free exercise!" Sound familiar? Many loathe hard work but love big results. Well, the reality, as you instinctively already know, is that anything worthy will take hard work. Don't push it away or avoid it. Rather, put it into the proper perspective — the hard work is temporary but the victory will last forever. The victories in your life that you are most proud of certainly came from those that you worked hardest for. Associate hard work with the feeling of accomplishment. Embrace it as part of your price for success.

By accepting the fact that hard work is a part of the process, you can now make one decision and be done with it.

That is, make a decision that that's it — whatever price you need to pay (as long as it is in alignment with your core values) you will simply pay it — without negotiation. For example, when I was in college we had to get up at 5 a.m. for swim practice. This was tough since typically I would wake up tired either from a lack of sleep, the hard training, or both. In addition it was generally dark and cold outside. I often wondered how I ended up in this sport given I didn't like to be either up early or cold. Regardless, I made one quality decision to get up and go to practice every morning no matter what. I could be dead tired or balls of hail the size of basketballs could be raining down but the decision was already made — I'm going. By doing this, I didn't have to go through the pain of remaking that decision each morning when I was most vulnerable to making the wrong choice. And so it went, the same routine every morning. The alarm would go off and I would get out of bed. My roommate would moan to me, "Hold on...I'm coming." However, there wouldn't be any movement from him and a minute later I'd hear, "No...go ahead this time. I'm staying in bed." Then, "Wait...I'm coming." Then, "No...I'm not." After a good five minutes of this I would head off to practice, sometimes with my roommate, sometimes without. The pain he went through each morning was excruciating to observe, let alone experience. Accepting that hard work was a necessary part of success. I was able to make one quality, non-negotiable decision. Managing that decision was more a matter of keeping a promise to myself than "gutting it up" with willpower like my roommate attempted. Without a doubt, I would have struggled at least as much as my roommate had I needed to make the decision each morning. However, by making that decision once I was able to act in spite of my feelings, not because of them. My actions were led by keeping a promise to myself. Since keeping a promise is all about integrity and honesty (two significant core values to me), it drove me more than my tiredness and aversion to being cold stopped me. Believe me, I'm as lazy as the next guy. I really don't see myself any more disciplined than anyone else. It is all a matter of how you set yourself up to win.

Finally, perseverance is increased simply by the understanding that it leads to habits. Habits lead us to do things naturally and effortlessly. Once it is a habit, the level of needed motivation and self-discipline goes way down as the "automatic pilot" takes over. Consequently, the object of perseverance becomes to keep the action going long enough until it becomes a habit, a way of life. Just as acting out of self-discipline may feel like you're a salmon swimming upstream (to stay on the swimming theme), acting out of our habits is like floating downstream with a current!

Develop – Supportive habits for long-term success.

It's been said, "You will never change your life until you change something you do daily." That's because what you do daily becomes a habit and we are creatures of our habits. Hence, the

> *The object of perseverance becomes to keep the action going long enough until it becomes a habit, a way of life.*

saying, "The secret to your success lies hidden in your daily routine." Think about it — most of us sleep on the same side of the bed each night, eat the same basic meals each week, and do the same general activities at often about the same time. We tend to park our car in the same places, sit in the same places, and meet with the same people about the same things. Simon Says! We quickly establish routines which develop habits and create comfort. Even our body language develops into a habit. For example, cross your arms. Now look down and notice which forearm is on top and which is on bottom.

> *"The secret to your success lies hidden in your daily routine."*

OK? Now, reverse it. Go ahead. Put the other arm on top. Does it feel comfortable or awkward? For most, it feels quite awkward as you are going against a well-engrained habit.

Our habits act as our automatic pilot. Without intervention, they will dictate our course in life with a powerful force. Ever try to break a bad habit? Tough, isn't it? That is the bad news. However, the good news is that same force applies to a good habit. Typically, we just don't notice the force of a good habit cause we are not pushing against it. It's like running in the wind. When you run against the wind, it is difficult and very tiring. It makes for a slow pace and it can be frustrating if you are trying to make good time. On the other hand, when the wind is at your back you hardly notice it. All you realize is that running feels exceptionally easy at the moment and you seem to be going much faster than normal. It is very relaxing and exciting at the same time.

The concept is to use the force of habits for good in your life. Get the "wind at your back." Determine what activity would be a good habit to have in your life and develop it. Get into action and stay there long enough to develop a habit. Typically, a habit begins to form in 30 days. And, fortunately, you can do just about anything for 30 days when you set your mind to it. How do you know when a habit is formed? You'll know because now you will be more drawn to do it than not to do it.

When setting your goals, it is important that you set achievable ones. As Vince Lombardi said, "Winning is a habit, but unfortunately so is losing." The concept is to **create a habit of achieving your goals.** Too often people develop a habit of not achieving goals because they are always too lofty. There is nothing wrong with a lofty goal but work your way to it. Set a lot of easy goals and hit them. Recognize yourself for it. Then, do it again, and again, and again. Soon your mind will create an expectancy for success with regards to goal achieving. At this point, raise the bar and repeat the process. Before you know it, your bar will be extremely high and you will have developed a solid habit of achieving the goals that you set.

> *"Winning is a habit, but unfortunately so is losing."*
> —*Vince Lombardi*

VISUALIZATION—Imaginary or Real?

In the early 1980s, I was first introduced to the concept of visualization. A sports psychologist was working with our U.S. Swim Team and taught us that training physically for our events was only part of the process. "You must prepare mentally for your victory as well as physically. You must first see and experience your victory in your mind's eye before you will ever see it in reality," he told us. "See, feel, and completely experience the victory in your mind many times over and you will manifest it," he added. I remember questioning the power of visualization, "Imaginary victories are important to success?" I questioned. "The key is understanding that imaginary victories (not friends) in your conscious mind are real to your subconscious mind. That is, your subconscious mind doesn't distinguish between imagined and real," he explained. By experiencing the victory over and over mentally, your subconscious accepts it as truth and does what it can to maintain the status quo — i.e., it attempts to 're-create' the victory in reality because it has "happened" so many times already.

> *"You must first see and experience your victory in your mind's eye before you will ever see it in reality."*

He drew out a very simple diagram called the Belief-Reality Graph. The concept was that we align what we believe to be true with reality. Henry Ford said, "Whether you believe you can do a thing or not, you are right." The work, therefore, in achieving goals is often in believing that you can do it. This is why pursuing goals that are aligned with our God-given Life Purpose is so important. Even the impossible becomes possible when God wills it. Consequently, it is truly a matter of believing and with God's will you can achieve it.

The graph works based on the principle that we like to be in balance. That is, we like having our reality to match what we believe to be true. That shouldn't be a surprise. Without such alignment, we feel tension. With a strong belief that our reality will change, the tension is felt positively as hope. However, as the belief drops, the tension morphs towards frustration, anxiety, despair and ultimately hopelessness.

In time, we will get back to the balance we naturally desire by one of two things happening:

1. We change our belief to match our current reality.
2. We experience the change in our reality that aligns with our belief.

For example in sports, if your time in an event was 1:00.00 (one minute even) but you believed you could do 58:00 (58 seconds), you are out of balance. There is a Belief – Reality Gap. Either you will achieve 58:00 or you will stop believing it. Similarly, in sales, you may believe you can hit certain numbers. And, again, either you will hit them or you will stop believing you can. The true work, therefore, is to maintain your belief long enough for your reality to catch up. However, the more you have visualized the success, the more your subconscious believes it to be true and the greater it will work to "re-create" it.

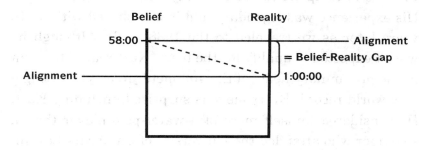

There are also times when your reality outperforms what you believe is possible. That is, something happens (e.g., you make more income, achieve more success, race faster than you believed you would) and you still can't believe it even though it happened. You think you must have been lucky or something. Consequently, you find yourself out of balance again, this time with your reality exceeding your belief. When this happens, either you will change your belief or else you will drop your reality through some form of self-sabotage. Have you ever seen someone who started succeeding but felt unworthy and then sabotaged their own success? It happens all the time. This is truly sad and unnecessary.

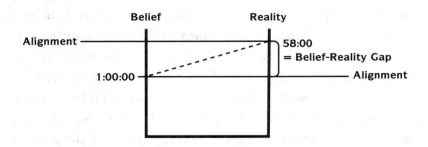

In 1972, American swimmer Kurt Krumplez traveled to Chicago to complete in the 1972 Olympic Swimming Trials. His experience was legendary and it was shared with us 16 years later as we traveled to the 1988 trials. Although he wasn't expected to qualify for the team, Kurt roared to a win in the preliminary heats of the 400-meter freestyle setting a new world record. Everyone was surprised, including Kurt. He considered himself more of a water-polo player than a swimmer who attended the University of California Los Angeles (UCLA). Between the preliminary heats and the finals that evening, he was left at a hotel for some eight hours to rest and prepare for the finals. He had far exceeded his expectations and the more time he had to think about it the more he talked himself out of what he had just done. By the time he reached the finals that evening, he wasn't mentally prepared to repeat the performance. As a result, he swam an equivalent time in the finals that he had done prior to his record setting effort of the morning. He placed sixth and did not qualify for the team. Further, he traveled to Munich, Germany and watched the race and awards presentation. He observed the gold medal be placed around the winner's neck without ever breaking Kurt's world record. (footnote — 36 years after Kurt's Olympic Trials swimming experience, his son J.W. earned a spot on the 2008 U.S. Olympic Water Polo team, winning an Olympic Silver medal.)

The visualization process begins by understanding that our imagination is truly connected to our physical being. During my visualization training, I was given a small thermometer that I held between my thumb and middle finger. The concept was to modify the temperature reading by changing the level of excitement in the mind. As the anxiety and excitement level increases, the body responds by bringing blood to the heart and large muscles as it prepares for the fight-or-flight response. As the blood leaves the fingertips, the temperature there goes down slightly yet measurably. This feedback was designed to establish the optimum level of positive stress. That is, there is a state whereby the body is prepared to perform optimally; not too anxious and not too relaxed.

> *The visualization process begins by understanding that our imagination is truly connected to our physical being.*

Next, we began visualizing our races as we wanted them to happen. The idea is to include all senses and emotions. Relax your body and close your eyes. Now visualize the event. See it. Feel it. Hear it. Smell it. Taste it. Completely experience it, emotionally and all. In our case with it being a timed event, we also included the real time with it. I recorded the race as it was designed to happen with the sound of a beep the exact moment I was to touch the wall on each turn of my race. As I visualized the race, my physiology changed. My heart rate increased, my blood flow changed, my muscle fibers fired, etc. To my body, it was real. I rehearsed the race over and over hearing the beep and turning in my mind. Remarkably, when I actually qualified for the 1988 Olympic Trials, my time was within one one-hundredth of a second to the time I had pre-recorded on my visualization "beeping" audio. One one-hundredth of a second is faster than the blink of an eye.

My coach Mike Troy said that he had pictured the Olympic gold medal being put around his neck countless times before his 1960 attempt. In fact, he always visualized the medal already having his name engraved onto its side when they gave it to him because it was destiny that he would win. There is a great photo of him on the awards platform of the 1960 Olympics in Rome. He is smiling with the gold medal around his neck. He was almost laughing because he had just looked at the side of the medal for his name when he realized that of course it wasn't engraved on it. He had simply pictured the victory (including his name on the side of the medal) so many times that he automatically turned the medal and looked for his name once he received it.

It doesn't matter if the topic is sports, business or relationships — the process is the same: "See it before you'll see it." Picture your success repeatedly and, consequently, become comfortable with your victory. This process will change your belief into expectancy. More often, you will achieve what you expect over what you want. Wanting something is nice, but expecting something is powerful. When you want success you will often *try* to achieve it. "Trying" to achieve success is like trying to describe the taste of salt; there is a whole lot of talk but not a lot of effective results. Even Yoda of the "Star Wars" movies says, "There is no try, only do." When you expect something, on the other hand, you are much more likely to do whatever that task requires to succeed.

When Disney World opened in Florida, there was a great

celebration. During the opening ceremony, the late Mrs. Walt Disney was told by a reporter, "Isn't it a shame that Walt isn't here to see this?" Mrs. Disney responded with, "The only reason why we are seeing the great opening is because long ago Walt already saw it."

AFFIRMATION – The Power of your words.
"Death and life are in the power of the tongue,..."
Proverbs 18:21

The final action step, in addition to physical and mental action, is taking verbal action. As the saying goes, "Confess it to possess it," or alternatively, we are "Hung by the tongue." Verify that what you say aligns with what you see and what you do in the pursuit of your goals. It doesn't make any sense to work hard to achieve something; visualize your successful victory, but say you can't do it all the while. Affirm your success. The Bible says, "Call forth those things that are not as if they were" (Romans 4:17). As discussed earlier, improve your self-talk. In addition, a powerful tool to help you achieve your goals is a written affirmation. Write out a description of your victory. What is happening? How are you feeling? Be descriptive and write it in the present tense as if you are currently living it. Read it often.

> *Verify that what you say aligns with what you see and what you do in the pursuit of your goals.*

For example, let's say you were making a presentation for business, charitable work or wherever, but you fear speaking in front of people. Your affirmation may be as simple as:

"I love giving presentations. When I speak in front of people, I feel confident and energized. I communicate clearly and passionately. People are interested in what I am saying. They ask questions and I comfortably and effectively answer them. The people I speak with are compelled by what I have to say and it results with [desired result]."

For many, a powerful addition to an affirmation is the addition of Scripture such as the previously mentioned verse, "I can do all things through Christ who strengthens me." (Phil. 4:13)

If you feel writing a positive affirmation seems odd or unhealthy for any reason I suggest you consider two things:

1. Is what you are affirming in alignment with your Life Purpose Statement? If it is in alignment, then affirming aspects of the fulfillment of that which you were designed to do is unarguably healthy. If it isn't in alignment, then adjust your affirmation such that it is.

2. You most likely have been repeatedly affirming statements of yourself and your future but they probably have just been the negative statements you are hearing in your mind, "I can't do it. I've never been good at this..." (Simon chatter) Yes, most people are comfortable with negative affirmations and, consequently, it is not the affirming part that seems odd, it's the positive version that most are not used to repeating.

Taking action towards your goals should incorporate the whole you. See it, say it, feel it and do it. Take action mentally by visualizing your success, verbally affirming it, and all the while feeling the victory. Then, take the physical action to bring it to reality. That is, when taking action, take action both mentally and physically. Specifically, lead with your mind, not your body. Too often, people say, "I'll believe it when I see it." Okay, then see it in your mind's eye first else you may never see it. Recently, a politician's slogan was, "He tells it like it is." Well, that isn't very exciting. I can see what is. Leadership and success comes from those who can see what can be and cast a vision to themselves and others. Action is a natural consequence at that point.

> *Most people are comfortable with negative affirmations and, consequently, it is not the affirming part that seems odd, it's the positive version that most are not used to repeating.*

A final note on taking action towards your goals is a reminder that anything worth achieving will take effort. People will often say that all this work is unnecessary and that if it is meant to be then God will provide. That perspective is simply an excuse for laziness. Yes, when you are in alignment with God and your Life Purpose, God will provide the resources; the inspiration, the people, etc. However, it still comes down to you choosing to take action.

A story is told of a great flood hitting a city. As the water started arriving at a man's house, a neighbor driving a jeep showed up and said, "Jump in and let's get out of here."

"No thank you. I'm fine. God will provide. God will save me," the man replied.

Later, with the water now flowing through the house, a rescue worker arrives in a boat and says, "Jump in and let's get out of here!"

"No thank you. I'm fine. God will provide. God will save me," the man replied.

Finally, the water now over the top of the man's house, he finds himself standing on his chimney when a helicopter arrives dropping a rope down for his rescue.

The man yells, "No thank you. I'm fine. God will provide.

God will save me."

The next thing the man knows he realizes that he is in heaven. He turns to God and asks, "Why didn't you provide? Why didn't you save me?"

God looked at him and said, "Why I did provide and I attempted to save you. Why didn't you get in the jeep, the boat, or grab the rope from the helicopter?"

God has provided your Life Purpose. He is also providing the way for you to fulfill it. The key is to take action on His plan! It is paramount that through introspection and revelation you have clarified a Life Purpose. With that, you now have something worthy of putting forth all the action possible — mentally and physically — to fulfill an inspired mission.

4. Review — Review the Results:

This step of your pattern is not only critically important but it is often the most common step omitted. People may access the situation, plan and prepare, and take action but often one of two things will follow: Either they will quit since "it isn't working," or they will keep doing the same thing over and over hoping for a better result. As you may have heard, the later action is clearly the definition of insanity — i.e., doing the same thing repeatedly expecting a different result. A third course of action is to review your results and make adjustments given the new data. Author John Maxwell puts it simply: "The pessimist complains about the wind. The optimist expects it to change. The leader adjusts the sails."

My college swim coach, Gregg Wilson, has gone down in the coaching history books with the NCAA record for most consecutive conference titles in any sport with 23 straight

Big West conference championships from 1979-2001. One of his greatest strengths was his regular review of results and consequent modifications. He would often start off his team meetings with the same phrase, "Well, we had some good swims and some not so good swims..." It was regular and predictable. In fact, often we would all say it together as he would start. The success of this approach is that the review was expected and, therefore, there was no real sting to it. Nobody was hurt by it. It was just part of the routine and a necessary component of success. We would praise and acknowledge the victories and we would learn together from the failures.

> "The pessimist complains about the wind. The optimist expects it to change. The leader adjusts the sails."
> —John Maxwell

Reviewing the results of any process should include both of these activities: Celebrate the victories and learn from the failures. However, since nobody likes to feel like a failure, often people avoid the reviewing of results in order to skip the revisiting of our failures.

Henry Cloud, psychologist, personal coach, and author of the book "Integrity," was performing a Q & A regarding raising children with successful character. A women raised her hand and asked, "If you could tell parents what the *one thing* is that is most important to teach their kids about success, what would it be?"

"I would teach them how to lose," he said.

The woman tilted her head, looked at him strangely, and said, "Why in the world would you want to teach them how to lose? After all, we were talking about success."

"Because *they will*," he said. (p. 159)

The challenge here is that we confuse failing with failure

and, consequently, not only do we not want to experience it, we don't even want to discuss it. Here is a big key: You are not a failure just because you failed. Ironically, the path to success is paved with failure. That is, successful people are not people who never fail. In fact, I have met several extremely successful people who have introduced themselves as their company's greatest "failures." Although they are having fun with their ironic humor, the point is well taken; those who hit the most home runs are often the ones who also strike out the most. In fact, if you literally look at baseball's Top 100 all time strikeout leaders, you will find names such as Reggie Jackson, Sammy Sosa, Jose Canseco, Mickey Mantle, Mark McGuire, Barry Bonds, Hank Aaron, Babe Ruth and others. Have you ever heard of them? Would you consider them baseball's failures? Success is not the avoidance of failure. Success is a matter of learning from failure, bouncing back and swinging again.

> *Success is not the avoidance of failure. Success is a matter of learning from failure, bouncing back and swinging again.*

How are successful people able to do this? First, they create a habit of looking for the lesson. Second, they bounce back by personally detaching themselves from the event itself.

The Lesson

A person's response to failure is one of the greatest distinctions between those who succeed and those who don't. When failure occurs, the average person naturally springs towards excuses or sympathy stories, while successful people go right to work on looking for the lesson. There is no value in simply complaining that something didn't go well. In fact, not only does it use energy, focus your mind on the failure, but it sets you up for a repeat performance since you didn't learn what to do differently next time (if there is a next time). Successful people are constantly learning, constantly striving to grow and understand that

> *A person's response to failure is one of the greatest distinctions between those who succeed and those who don't.*

often their best lessons reside in their failures.

Failure is a tool. It is something that you learn from. There is always a lesson hidden in your failure — what is it? If after you grab the lesson, aren't you one step closer to success? With this new knowledge you didn't previously have, aren't your odds of succeeding the next time better than before? If so, then who's to say that wasn't a valuable event in your life? It may not have been enjoyable or desirable, but it was valuable. Remember, you fail forward.

> *Successful people are constantly learning, constantly striving to grow and understand that often their best lessons reside in their failures.*

Is it possible to succeed all the time? Absolutely. Why not consider a valuable event as just described as a successful one? That is, when you take a lesson away from an event, you have grown and are in a better position to succeed than before. Therefore, by equating value with success, you can rewrite the rules by which you operate. This may seem like logical rhetoric but once understood and accepted, the concept may well change your life. Consider changing the standard definition of success to the new definition listed on the following page.

Standard Definition of Success:
- Success = Achievement of Goal
- Failure = Failure to achieve Goal

New Definition of Success:
- Success = Achievement of Goal -OR- Success = Failure to achieve Goal + Lesson learned
- Failure = Failure to achieve Goal without a lesson learned

With the new definition of success, the only way to fail is to not learn! In other words, if you are always looking for the lesson, then whether you achieve the goal or not becomes secondary. With constant learning, it is only a matter of time until you realize success. In addition, this new perception should add to your ability to persevere. It is much easier to believe, and rightfully so, that you will achieve success when you make an adjustment thanks to a lesson learned. Although you may not feel the excitement of achieving your goal, you do have the added confidence of new knowledge and, therefore, a greater expectation of coming success.

> *It is much easier to believe, and rightfully so, that you will achieve success when you make an adjustment thanks to a lesson learned.*

On May 29, 1953, Sir Edmund Hillary was the first man to summit Mount Everest. At 29,000 feet, it is the tallest point on earth. However, he didn't achieve this accomplishment on his first attempt. In fact, in 1952 a few weeks after a failed attempt, he was addressing a group of people in England. During his talk, he walked to the edge of the platform, made a fist and pointed at a picture of the mountain. He said in a loud voice, "Mount Everest, you beat me the first time, but I'll beat you the next time because you've grown all you are going to grow...but I'm still growing!" He knew that his lessons would inevitably lead to overcoming the mountain itself.

The Detachment

The ability to "bounce-back" from failure also greatly distinguishes those who succeed and those who don't. Unless you plan on succeeding the first attempt every time, having the ability to "bounce-back" from failing to achieve your goal is crucial. We have all heard the simple saying, "If at first you don't succeed, try, try again." That is easier said than done unless you have learned the secret of detachment. Detachment is simply the process of disconnecting yourself from the actual activity.

Often, people mistakenly associate *what they are doing* with *who they are.* We have already discussed this concept, but it plays a big role at this point in success. When you associate what you are doing with who you are, you personalize everything that happens. That is, your *being* becomes dependent upon the results of your *doing.* When the re-

> *Often, people mistakenly associate what they are doing with who they are.*

sults are good, you are good. When the results are bad, you are bad. The key here is to detach yourself from the event. When you personalize the event, YOU feel like the failure. When you detach yourself from the event, you feel like the EVENT was a failure. This distinction is a major one. If YOU failed, it can really hurt emotionally and be difficult to bounce back from. If the EVENT failed, it is not so personal. Simply learn from it and move on. Consequently, you aren't necessarily down just because your results are. How do you bounce back quickly? Never fall too far down in the first place by not personalizing the failure.

Consider the following quote by Thomas Edison from an interview published in the January 1921 issue of American Magazine; I think that was in black and white. "After we had conducted thousands of experiments on a certain project without solving the problem, one of my associates, after we had conducted the crowning experiment and it had proved a failure, expressed discouragement and disgust over our having failed to find out anything. I cheerily assured him that we had learned something. For we had learned for a certainty that the thing couldn't be done that way, and that we would have to try some other way."

Thomas Edison understood the difference between an experiment failing and personally failing. This clearly defined separation between the two, and gave him the great advantage of being able to readily bounce back with more experiments. As a result, we all enjoy the ramifications of his success today.

After detaching yourself from the outcome of the event, further increase your emotional stability by detaching from the belief that the results will never change. That is, reality says sometimes the event will go well, sometimes it won't. By acknowledging this truth, you have now tempered your emotions. You won't be surprised when things go well nor when they do not because you understand that it is all part of the process of achievement. Now, don't misunderstand, I'm not suggesting that you don't visualize, affirm, and expect successful results. Of course you should! The idea is to do everything you can to succeed yet understand that sometimes you will hit your mark and sometimes you will not.

Get used to saying, "And this too shall pass..." I have used this phrase a lot, particularly in business, to establish a long-term bounce-back ability. When things are not going well..."And this too shall pass." I'll remind myself and others that the poor results we are experiencing will pass and we'll be getting great results again. However, even when things are going extremely well... "And this too shall pass." Yes, it seems pessimistic and I'm not suggesting that you project on-coming doom for yourself; however, I am suggesting that just as things won't always be bad, they won't always be perfect either. This connection with reality will help motivate you to stay sharp during the good times and it will be valuable to you when you are looking forward to bouncing back after a tough time. As mentioned earlier, the bounce-back isn't too difficult if you never fall far down in the first place.

The Process

Review the progress of your goals every 30 days. The time-line is important. First, it is easier to think of activity in 30 day, bite-size efforts than to think about it for a matter of months or years. It is a lot less intimidating. When you think about a goal that will take a year or more, for example, many people will immediately be overwhelmed and depressed by the thought. "How will I ever do that?" It's just sometimes too much for the mind to handle; baby steps. However, when it is put into a 30-day segment, it is not nearly as daunting. You can stay the course for 30 days. When people ask me about my extreme running, the question is often, "How do you run so far [100 mile+]?" My response is that I don't run 100+

miles. I run one mile, 100+ times. Sometimes it is even more bite size as in one step many, many times over. I was taught that during such races to never think about how far you still have to go as it will depress you and cause you to feel tired just by the thought of it. I was also taught never to think about how far you've gone as when you ponder that — it also will cause you to feel tired as you think about what you have done. Instead, think about the now — the next step, the next breath. In life, stay focused on the 30-day effort. The past is over and the future has not happened yet so by focusing your energy on the now, you don't get tired from the things that aren't really happening.

The second reason for setting the review for every 30 days is that this is the timeline that develops habits. As new habits develop, you may well find that the needed effort (self-discipline) decreases. The "pulling" force of a habit is always a great relief from the "pushing" force of self-discipline. That is, a habit pulls you to do what previously your self-discipline had to push you to do. Consequently, you may well look at the effort towards a goal differently with new habits now assisting. Since you will likely find that you can do more than you could 30 days earlier, it would be the right time to update your plan. On the flip side, if a habit isn't forming, now would be the time to question why.

> *A habit pulls you to do what previously your self-discipline had to push you to do.*

A final reason that is important to review every 30 days is in case you are off course. If you are off course, you will have caught it early enough that it can be corrected. An airplane that is flying by automatic pilot is very slightly off course most all of the time. The flying conditions cause it to be heading in one direction or the other slightly too much throughout the flight. However, with very regular checks and corrections, it is unnoticeable to the passenger and the plane predictably arrives at its intended destination. You will almost always be slightly off course as well. That's fine. It's part of the journey. The key is to check and adjust early and regularly enough so that you too will arrive at your intended destination.

Review your 30 days by asking various questions: What did you learn? What worked? What didn't work? Review all areas of your plan and not just your action portion. That is, review all five areas of your plan as defined in your "Aim" section above to consider the effectiveness of each component.

5. Repeat — Repeat the Process

Congratulations! You have completed a cycle! Now, it's time to begin again. However, this time you have the experience of the last cycle to guide you and prepare you for even better results! Reassess yourself. Redefine your gap. Update your plan and prepare for success. Imagine how much further along you will be as you get sharper every 30 days. Imagine as you grow how much more you can expect to see successful results. Imagine the difference in your results as compared to just taking action without any regular reflection and refinement.

CHAPTER 19

Results

*However beautiful the strategy, you should
occasionally look at the results.*
–Winston Churchill

BELIEF SYSTEM ➤ EMOTIONS ➤ ATTITUDE ➤ ACTIONS ➤ **RESULTS**

> *The results in your
> life are directly
> related to the quality
> of the decisions that
> you make.*

> *With your Life Purpose
> Statement as your
> guide, develop your
> belief system, your
> emotional intelligence,
> your attitudes, and
> your actions, and
> your life will be a
> masterpiece.*

The results in your life are directly related to the quality of the decisions that you make. That is, if you want better results in your life, make better decisions. To make better decisions consider the input that directs your thinking. The better the input, the better the decisions, the better the life...for everyone. The first step in improving the results in your life is to take responsibility for them. Your future is not dependent upon your past, but rather dependent upon your decisions of today. If you want to change the past, change today because today will be tomorrow's past. Did you get that?

With your Life Purpose Statement as your guide, develop your belief system, your emotional intelligence, your attitudes, and your actions, and your life will be a masterpiece. Remember, it doesn't need to all happen in a day. The key is that you are growing. You are either getting better or worse; nobody stays the same. In fact, the comment, "You know, you haven't changed at all," may be flattering when it comes to appearance or certain positive qualities but it isn't what you want to hear when it comes to personal and spiritual growth.

Section 4

Fulfilling Your Life Purpose

FREEDOM FROM THE ANCHORS OF LIFE

CHAPTER 20

Start & Don't Stop

If one advances confidently in the direction of his dreams, and endeavors to live the life, which he has imagined, he will meet with a success unexpected in common hours.
−Henry David Thoreau

It is an amazing process to realize that you were truly born for a reason. The whole concept of discovering a Life Purpose and a meaningful direction for your life is beyond measurable value. However, what would be the point in discovering your Life Purpose, gaining tools to pursue it, yet never understanding how to release the anchor of your ship allowing you to actually set sail once and for all to actually fulfill it? How frustrating! Consequently, this section is all about releasing those anchors and freeing yourself to truly fulfill your Life Purpose.

When I was 23 years old I had my first opportunity to get business counsel from who later became my financial mentor, Dan Williams. When we first met, I remember trying to decide what deep question I should ask him. Finally, I just said, "What is the one piece of advice you could give me that, more than anything else, would help me succeed?" I was excited to hear his longwinded answer. I knew it would be profound, deep and really complicated. He certainly had the fruit on the tree and I knew he was filled with wisdom. However, his answer was short and simple. At first it made no sense to me. He said, "You want the secret to success?"

"Yes!" I replied almost panting like a puppy. "What is it?" I asked again thinking I should tape record his reply (dating myself again).

"Okay. Here it is: Start and don't stop," he said.

"Start and don't stop?" I replied back with a frown and a questioning tone.

"Absolutely," he said. "Start towards your dream and don't ever stop."

I remember leaving him that evening shaking my head, "What's with 'Start and don't stop'?" I didn't understand how profound his statement to me really was.

Over the years, I've come to realize that in order to start anything it takes faith. It takes faith just to get out of bed in the morning and begin a new day. It takes faith to drive on the freeways (especially here in Southern California!). It takes faith to begin a new relationship or start a new task.

> *Allow yourself the ability to rediscover and reinvent yourself as you focus forward and fulfill your Life Mission.*

The greater the journey, typically the greater the faith it takes to start. For many, starting something can be the most difficult part. In order to accomplish your Life Mission of fulfilling your Life Purpose, extraordinary faith will need to be called upon. It should be necessary since, after all, what journey is greater than accomplishing your Life Mission?

The statement, however, wasn't just to "Start." It was, "Start and don't stop." In order to not stop, you must experience freedom from the things that hold you back. It is essential to be free from past programming, past experiences, and past resentments. It is essential to be free from the negative or controlling influence of others and it is essential to be free from the control of our own ego. Allow yourself the ability to rediscover and reinvent yourself as you focus forward and fulfill your Life Mission.

CHAPTER 21

Faith

*Faith is putting all your eggs in God's basket, then
counting your blessings before they hatch.*
–Ramona C. Carroll

"What's at the center of your life?" The answer to this
question will tell quite a story about you. Too often people
have centered their life around certain people, work, leisure,
lifestyle, entertainment, or material success. It isn't just a
part of their life, it is at the center of their life. The challenge
is how do you truly fulfill something when your life revolves
around something else? Or, considered another way, how is
it that the people, work or whatever you have at the center
of your life are able to fulfill you? Unfortunately, they won't
and shouldn't be expected to. Rather, they are designed to
play a supportive role. Your fulfillment in life will be directly
related to the fulfillment of your Life Purpose. Consequently,
what if you put your Life Purpose and the one who gave it to
you at the center of your life? By doing so, you have just put
the two things in the center of your life that can't be taken
away from you.

Your faith in God and your Life Purpose are yours to keep.
Everything else are simply gifts — be grateful for them. Let

your creator fulfill you and release that responsibility from other people and things. Of course, I'm not suggesting that we don't need other people in our lives — we do. We are very much relational beings. However, by focusing on fulfillment through faith-based and on-purpose living rather than solely through other people and things, it not only provides ultimate fulfillment but security and freedom as well. That is, since faith in God and your Life Purpose cannot be taken from you, your fulfillment is secure and ongoing. It also frees you to serve others rather than living in constant need to be served.

In other words, you can clearly apply your purpose to all areas of your life including family, friends, work, and so on. Your journey in life can now switch from receiving to serving, similarly to what John F. Kennedy said in his 1961 inaugural address: "Ask not what your country can do for you — ask what you can do for your country." A spiritually centered life will allow you to grow in dramatic ways, give you peace during the turbulent times of your journey, and empower you to fulfill your Life Mission.

> *A spiritually centered life will allow you to grow in dramatic ways, give you peace during the turbulent times of your journey and empower you to fulfill your Life Mission.*

It is possible that this may cause some readjustment in your life. If you have been leaning on others and things to fulfill you, give you peace and happiness, then this adjustment will achieve what it is that you have desired all along. That is, you will enjoy true joy, peace and happiness by being connected with your creator and living an on-purpose life. There is a concept in hypnotherapy called the law of reverse effect which in simple terms means the harder you try the more difficult it becomes. By setting joy, peace and happiness as the goal, the more elusive it becomes. However, by focusing on living a life in faith and on purpose, then joy, peace and happiness are natural byproducts. That is, do not seek these results directly but rather enjoy them as they come to you as a result of doing that which produces them.

THE FAITH TO SURRENDER

Surrender. Just surrender. For many of us the word "surrender" doesn't sit well. In fact, we feel the instant fight build up inside as our ego wants to maintain control. Our ego says, "I'm in charge. Never surrender!" However, in order to become who you can be, you must first be willing to surrender to something greater than your ego. What you surrender to has power over you. If you stay surrendered to your ego, it will rule your life. Not only will you be limited, but you will often be fighting the wrong battles. Your ego wants to be "right" and it wants to "win" — and, it will fight for those victories. However, when you surrender to God and allow faith to center you, you will quickly see the higher power available to change your life. You will find your life isn't about being "right" or "winning" but about "peace" and "purpose."

Anyone recovering from an addiction will understand that the first step of recovery is to surrender; understanding that you don't have power over the thing that is controlling you. Although most people think of addition as being simply drugs, alcohol, pornography or some other highly publicized vice, challenging emotional states such as worry, pride, envy, anxiety and others can also become addictive ways of thinking driven primarily by the ego. When you try to beat these thoughts personally, you will most likely find out just how limited you really are. When you look to a greater source than yourself, you will find tremendous strength. Ironically, dropping to your knees is very empowering. There's a poem that's associated with A.A. called "Dry as a Camel."

> *Ironically, dropping to your knees is very empowering.*

The camel each day goes twice to his knees;
He picks up his load with the greatest of ease;
He goes through the day with his head held high;
And he stays for that day completely dry.

As the saying goes, "Let go and let God." A friend of mine said to me a long time ago, "Why are you carrying the weight of the world around on your shoulders? Give it to God; he's got a really big set of shoulders." And so I did, and what a relief! Similarly, but on an obviously smaller scale, I remember when I finally got tired of not getting the results I wanted in business and I turned to my mentor and surrendered control. I said, "OK, you take the lead...I'll follow your direction." I had to have faith that he had superior knowledge, a plan, and that it would all work out. It did. Have faith that your creator has superior knowledge, a plan for your life, and that it will all work out as well. He does.

This concept is not a shunning of responsibility as some may quickly assume. Rather, it is acknowledging that which you can handle yourself and that which is beyond your ability and simply giving it to a higher power. As the "Serenity Prayer" says:

God, grant me the serenity to accept the things I cannot

change; the courage to change the things I can; and the wisdom to know the difference.

> To truly fulfill your Life Purpose, remove your ego and your control from the center of your life and replace it with your Life Purpose and your relationship with God.

Remove your ego and your control from the center of your life and replace it with your Life Purpose and your relationship with God. No longer will you depend upon your abilities but rather on His. As Stephen Covey says, "Whatever is at the center of our life will be the source of our security, guidance, wisdom, and power." Suddenly, your impossible mission of fulfilling your Life Purpose is not only possible but probable.

THE FAITH TO OVERCOME WORRY

Worry runs ramped in our society. We worry about everything from whether we will get the job we just interviewed for to what others think about us to what the day will bring our way. Some worries have a seed of reality to them and some do not even have that...yet, we still worry. Consider the following story of a goose in a bottle:

There was a teacher that asked her class to imagine that they put a goose egg into a bottle. When the goose egg hatched, the baby goose began to grow. The assignment was to figure out how to get the goose out without breaking the bottle or injuring the goose. The following day the students returned to the class. One student admitted to not being able to sleep as he wrestled all night with the dilemma without coming up with the answer. "How do we get the goose out?!"

he demanded to know. The teacher said, "Very well. Bring me the bottle with the goose inside and I will show you." To that the students suddenly realized that they have been struggling with something that did not actually exist; you can't get a goose egg into a bottle. And, so it is with the things that you worry about...most often they either they don't really exist or they are beyond your ability to change.

Have the faith to overcome worry. Remember, your creator didn't create you for harm. That makes no sense. If He can create the universe, He can certainly help guide you through your part in it. In fact, as referenced earlier, the Bible says in Romans 8:28, "And we know that God causes all things to work together for good to those who love God, to those who are called according to His purpose." Our worry is evidence of our lack of faith. Between having faith that God will fulfill this promise and living according to the "Serenity Prayer," peace will replace your worry.

> *Our worry is evidence of our lack of faith.*

THE FAITH TO FOLLOW YOUR INTUITION

Years ago, I asked my mentor Dan Williams, "What is the most important skill for me to develop?" I thought he might say, "people skills," or "negotiation skills," or "systematic thinking," or something I had worked on. Once again, however, I was surprised by his answer: "Intuition." He said, "Developing your ability to follow your intuition is your most important skill. There is endless knowledge to gain, but all the while your intuition will guide you."

Your intuition is the direct perception of truth independent of any reasoning process. It's what you know in your heart to be true or a "gut instinct" that is speaking to you. Have you ever done something and, only afterwards, said, "I knew I shouldn't have done that"? When taking an exam, we have all heard, "Go with your first answer." Why? — Because our intuition is powerful.

In Malcolm Gladwell's book, "Blink," he recounts a story of an art dealer by the name of Gianfranco Becchina who, in 1983, approached the J. Paul Getty Museum in California with a statue. The statue was known as a Kouros; a sculpture of a nude male youth dating back to the sixth century BC. There are only about 200 of Kouroi in existence, and this one was nearly perfectly preserved! Becchina was asking just under $10 million for it.

The Getty took the statue on loan and moved cautiously, attempting to assure its authenticity. Questions were asked about its origin. Experts were hired to perform scientific tests on the stone itself. Everything checkout out and after 14 months of due diligence, the Getty was convinced and purchased the Kouros.

The purchase was made in spite of several experts sharing their "feelings" that it didn't look right. Italian art historian Federico Zeri, who served on the Getty's board of trustees, took his first look at it and said the sculpture's fingernails "seemed wrong" to him. He couldn't articulate why. Evelyn Harrison, a foremost expert on Greek sculpture, took one look at the sculpture and knew it was amiss. She was told, "Well, it isn't ours yet but it will be in a couple of weeks." To that, she responded, "I'm sorry to hear that." She couldn't explain why — she only had a hunch. Thomas Hoving, the former director of the Metropolitan Museum of Art in New York, always makes a note of the first word that goes through his head when he sees something new. When he first looked at the statue, the word "Fresh," went through his mind. Considering the statue was reportedly some 2,000 years old, "fresh" wasn't necessarily an appropriate word. "Have you paid for this?" he asked. "If you have, try to get your money back. If you haven't, don't."

The above experts knew in a glance what the Getty team of lawyers and scientists couldn't discover in 14 months of investigation. Their "intuitive repulsion" was all that was needed to render their instant conclusion.

In order to fulfill your Life Purpose, you will need to become an "expert" of your own life and learn to follow your intuition over what Simon says. It is essential that you gain wisdom and insight about who you are and what you are doing in life in order to become such an expert. This is why a focus on God's wisdom and will for your life is so important. Regularly remind yourself to surrender your ego, pray for wisdom, and seek guidance and clarity. With this preparation, when the moment calls for it, you will be ready to depend on your intuition and not Simon's. Learn to look to it and trust that small, still voice that speaks to you.

> *In order to fulfill your Life Purpose, you will need to become an 'expert' of your own life and learn to follow your intuition over what Simon says.*

FAITH'S FUEL: QUIET TIME - RESTORATION & REVELATION

Trust GOD from the bottom of your heart; don't try to figure out everything on your own. Listen for God's voice in everything you do, everywhere you go; He's the one who will keep you on track. Prov. 3:5-6 (Msg)

It's been said, "It's the space between the notes that makes the music." Without the quiet space, the beauty of the music couldn't be heard. And, it's the time of quiet reflection between life's activities that revels the truth. In order to gain clarity of purpose and direction in your life, you must slow down enough to receive it.

I know how difficult it can be for people (particularly men) to stop and ask directions when driving somewhere. As the joke goes, why are there 100 million sperm to fertilize one egg? Answer: because not one of those little guys would stop to ask for directions. However, there hopefully comes a point in one's life where you are able to set the ego aside, stop driving a million miles an hour in every direction, and consider the value of getting clarity on where you are going — tell Simon to take a break.

Imagine you're driving along a road and someone says something to you as you zoom by. Would you even notice? Probably not. Of course, if you crashed and that individual came up to your car and spoke to you, you would probably notice now, wouldn't you? And so is life. We are zooming around non-stop. Our egos are chattering away loudly in our head. We're too busy debating with imaginary conversations to take a moment for some quiet time. There is a small, still voice attempting to guide you, inform you and inspire you. Do you hear it? Can you make some time to listen or will you only make that time after you have "crashed" in life?

Believe me, I understand running fast and hard without time to stop. Even knowing the importance of slowing down and having some quiet time didn't seem to make a difference. For me, I had to come to a crash in life in order for my quiet time to begin. Can you relate?

Here is a great related principle from an old story of a woodcutter:

Once upon a time there was a very strong woodcutter who was determined to do his best on a new job. His boss gave him an axe and showed him where to work.

The first day, the woodcutter brought in 18 trees. "Congratulations," the boss said. "That is excellent work!" Very motivated by the boss' words, the woodcutter put in an even greater effort the next day, but he could only bring in 15 trees. On the third day, he tried even harder, but he could only bring in 10 trees.

Day after day he was bringing in less and less trees. "I must be losing my strength," the woodcutter thought. He went to the boss and apologized, saying that he could not understand what was going on.

"When was the last time you sharpened your axe?" the boss asked."Sharpen? I haven't had time to sharpen my axe. I've been too busy trying to cut down these trees!"

The question is will you make sharpening your axe part of your daily routine? Please don't say you are too busy chopping down the trees of life. There comes a point when we must all recognize that it really makes more sense to take the

> *There comes a point when we must all recognize that it really makes more sense to take the time to sharpen ourselves rather than grinding down to a totally ineffective state.*

time to sharpen ourselves rather than grinding down to a totally ineffective state. Abraham Lincoln understood this principle as he said, "If I had eight hours to chop down a tree, I'd spend six sharpening my axe!"

Through quiet time you can experience both **restoration** and **revelation**. The result is transforming. Not only will restoration allow you to sharpen your axe and bring it back to the fresh sharpness that it once was, but through revelation you can become sharper than ever before.

Restoration is the renewing of one's self. The Bible refers to renewing your mind when it says, "And do not be conformed to this world, but be transformed by the renewing of your mind...(Romans 12:2). Conforming to the world often leads one to "losing their mind" not "renewing" it. Remember, be transformed by the renewal of your mind, not the removal of it.

Restoration isn't about being idle. It is about activities that renew your mind, heart and soul. Restoration occurs differently for everyone. President Ronald Reagan would fly to his Santa Barbara, Calif. ranch, ride horses, clear trails and chop wood. Think about it, the leader of the free world, while battling the Cold War and orchestrating the duties of being president, would break and chop wood. Similarly, Winston Churchill, amidst a raging world war, would sit quietly for hours and paint landscapes. President Abraham Lincoln would read humor books.

People who achieve great heights understand the importance of restoration. Whether it is hiking, gardening, or some other activity, it is important to discover and regularly perform that which gives you restoration.

Personally, I enjoy running in the remote mountains. Unless you're a deer, that may seem odd, but for me it is relaxing and renewing.

Revelation is the revealing or disclosing of God's will for your life along with other forms of wisdom and understanding. In order for revelation to occur, take time to praise God for your blessings, and ask for wisdom, guidance and inspiration. Then, remember to listen.

Meditate on what is important to you. Remember, mediation simply means to give serious thought to something. Worry is a form of mediation. Perhaps you have some experience? When you meditate, you are thinking of a thought over and over and from every angle. Perhaps it is time to meditate on what you want instead of what you don't want. Perhaps it is time to mediate on what your Creator desires and for which He has uniquely designed you.

Make quiet time a priority. Determine when, where and how you will work it into your daily routine. Then, enjoy your transformation!

CHAPTER 22

Freedom

I know but one freedom and that is the freedom of the mind.
—Antoine de Saint-Exupery

Step one of fulfilling your Life Purpose: "Start'" by Faith. Step two: "Don't Stop" by experiencing Freedom from the things that hold you back. We are held back by the experiences of our past, by the influence of others, and by our own ego. Yet, once we are aware of this, we can redefine ourselves in order to stay the course and experience our victory.

FREEDOM FROM THE PAST:

The first step toward becoming free from your past is to acknowledge where its place is in your life. The past lives behind you and is best described with the metaphor of a boat's wake. When you look at a boat, the wake is behind it. The wake does not power the boat. The wake does not steer the boat. The wake is simply the evidence, the remaining results of the boat's presence. By studying the wake, you can learn a lot about the boat but it clearly doesn't power it, direct it or define it.

Your past has simply been a result of the choices that you

and others have made; the better the choices, the better the results. And, although the results in your life are extremely important, even more so are the meanings you assigned to them. Everything that has happened in your life, starting as a young child, you assigned meaning to and, consequently, this process has shaped your view of the world. Therefore, your environments and the experiences you encountered do not make you. Rather, everything depends on what you make of it; the meaning you assign to it. As Anthony Robbins says, "It's not the events of our lives that shape us, but our beliefs as to what those events mean." As a result, your perception is your reality. Perception, however, is not in stone. It is changeable. Want to change the world? Begin with changing the way you see it. Start with the way you see yourself.

> *Your environments and the experiences you encountered do not make you. Rather, everything depends on what you make of it; the meaning you assign to it.*

> *Want to change the world, begin with changing the way you see it. Start with the way you see yourself.*

Ironically, to be free from the past you must first embrace it. You cannot sweep it under the carpet, put your head in the sand or any other activity that represents the utter ignoring of it. It must be faced. As Dr. Phil says, "You've got to face it to replace it." Accept responsibility for the choices that you have made. If you are not happy with your life, accept responsibility for it. If you don't like your job, where you live, or your financial situation, accept responsibility for it. Don't take a victim role. Nothing can be resolved when you blame others. Rather than making excuses for your life, embrace the reality of what it has been and the responsibility for the choices that you have made.

This process may be particularly difficult when you have been dealt a difficult hand. However, it is still important that you accept the responsibility of, at minimum, the choice of attitude and meaning assigned to the events of your life. A good personal friend of mine, Tom Jones, was physically and sexually abused as a baby and young boy. His brother also endured the same physical abuse. His childhood was horrific and something nobody should have ever experienced. From long-term sexual abuse to enduring hot cigarette butts being put out on his tender skin, it is amazing that either he or his brother even survived. They both did but with very different results. Tom is now a motivational speaker who works regularly with abused and abandoned children while his brother is in jail. Tom believes that his horrible experience was valuable as it gave him the means to connect with children in a way that others simply can't. In fact, his ability to empathize with the children one on one as well as his ability to stir the soul of adults as he tells his story has positively impacted countless people. His brother, unfortunately, remains angry and bitter which continues to bring unpleasant consequences today. The difference is their choice of attitude regarding their past and the meaning they have assigned to it.

Victor Frankl wrote, "We who lived in concentration camps can remember the men who walked through the huts comforting others, giving away their last piece of bread. They may have been few in number, but they offer sufficient proof that everything can be taken from a man but one thing: the last of human freedoms — to choose one's attitude in any given set of circumstances — to choose one's own way."

Once you attempt to choose the right attitude and assign

the right meaning to the events of our past, many still struggle with shame and guilt over them. Shame and guilt lead to irrational thoughts such as, "I am an awful person for that to have happened to me," or "I do not deserve to be happy." These bad feelings of one's self often then lead to a desire for an abundance of accolades as medicine to cover up the internal hurt. Unfortunately, there are never enough accolades to fully numb the hurt and the past is now clearly brought into the present. Finally, because hurting people hurt people, a new negative cycle begins again in the present. Each negative cycle reinforces the original bad feelings which entrenches them even deeper. The result: It's a domino effect of difficulties through life. We're not talking pizza here! This is real life and it's tough.

Consequently, a decision must be made that it is now time to let it go. You have embraced your past, learned what you can from it, and now it is time to box it up and let it go. Don't let your bad feelings trick you into believing that you deserve a difficult or unhappy life. That's ridiculous and nobody is helped by it. Rather, accept responsibility of your past and also the freedom from it as you allow yourself the liberty of beginning anew. Again, to refer to Frankl, "It is a privilege of man to become guilty and his responsibility to overcome guilt. Man does not have the freedom to undo what he has done, but he does have the freedom to choose the right attitude to guilt. A man who has failed by a deed cannot change what happened, but by repentance he can change himself."

Through the process of accepting responsibility of our lives and of the choices that we have made, much of the blame that we have assigned to others will shift to ourselves. Consequently, we will blame others less, but we will still blame others. The final step of freedom from our past is to not only liberate ourselves from our past but others as well. That is, just as we must release ourselves from the shame and guilt resulting from that which we blame ourselves, we must also be released from the resentment that results from that which we blame others. As the saying goes, "It is not the snake bite, but the venom that runs throughout the body, that kills." Shame, guilt and resentment are all venomous and must go in order for you to be free.

Some people have an easier time forgiving themselves than they do others. Other people are just the opposite. Regardless, forgiveness is a catalyst and a necessity for a positive, productive future. Blame is the parking brake to growth. After you have embraced and learned from the challenges of your past, forgive — yourself and others. Perhaps you struggle to show someone forgiveness. Perhaps they don't deserve it. Now what? Understand that forgiveness is not about justice. Your resentment towards another person only sends venom through your body; not through theirs. So, who is hurt by your unwillingness to forgive? You. Consequently, if you can't forgive them for their sake than at least do it for your own. Remember, the bite is over — let the venom end as well.

However, as you grow, strive to treat people not as they deserve but as you are. That doesn't mean you aren't standing on principle and that there aren't consequences for one's choices. Rather, it means you can treat people with love not because they deserve it, but because you are loving. You can forgive people not because they deserve forgiveness, but because you are forgiving. Your ability to serve another is no longer dependent upon who they are, but rather on who you are.

Christians have a great advantage in the area of forgiveness. Through the Christian worldview, we understand that regardless of how unworthy we are to receive a perfect God's forgiveness for our sins, he forgives us anyway through Christ. Consequently, it is God's grace that affords the Christian no option but to forgive others as he himself has been forgiven. How can we receive forgiveness from God and yet not pass on forgiveness to our fellow man? To the Christian, it would be pure hypocrisy. This process of forgiveness towards others was exemplified by Christ himself as he hung dying on the cross. Rather than cursing and resenting those who were crucifying him, he specifically sought their forgiveness as he said to God, "Father, forgive them; for they know not what they do" (Luke 23:34).

FREEDOM FROM OTHERS:

Without being aware of it, many people are living "Outside-In" rather than "Inside-Out." That is, rather than living according to your own Core Values, purpose and assignment (that which is inside), you are living according to what Simon has defined for you (that which is outside).

> *Without being aware of it, many people are living "Outside-In" rather than "Inside-Out.".*

Outside-in living is backwards. You are living according to what Simon says you should do, have, and be. "You should…" begins the advice-giving statement: "You should try this… You should do that… You should have a… You should be more…" In fact, at times it can be difficult to keep up with all of the "Shoulds" that people throw at us! As mentioned earlier, "Don't let people "should" on you." Although some of the should statements are actually good, helpful and would be wise to incorporate into our life, the key is not to automatically live by all of them.

A close cousin of the "should" is the "can't" statement. "Can't" statements are what others say you can and cannot achieve. Often, they are hidden in a "should" statement, such as "You shouldn't...[because you can't]." By accepting others' "can't" statements, you again are allowing others to define your life for you. Again, consider them; just don't automatically accept them.

Finally, most of us have people who can "push our buttons" emotionally. In-laws? They seem to have the ability to light us up at will and as a result show an extraordinary control over us. When a button-pusher is effective enough, we may not only feel different emotionally but even physically inside as we experience the literal effects of outside-in living.

Whether you seem to be surrounded by advice givers and button pushers or whether you only experience it once in a while, it is time to turn it around and live inside-out. It is time to live your own life.

Freedom From Others: Advice Givers

Have you ever heard the saying, "Those who know the least, know it the loudest!"? Why is it that those without the fruit on the tree often insist on boldly giving their unsolicited advice? It is dangerous advice because it often comes with the sound of great authority. Yet, if you look at the results that their thinking has produced in their own life, it usually doesn't make sense to follow their advice. However, that doesn't stop most people from giving you their unbridled opinion. Yes, people love to tell you what they think especially when it comes to what you should do, have, or become.

Have you noticed there are a lot of experts out there when the subject of discussion is you? Ironically, when the advice actually is good sound counsel, often these advice givers are not even following it themselves or "practicing what they preach." Hence, the saying, "Take my advice, I'm not using it." The key question is what are you doing with the advice you are given?

> *"Take my advice, I'm not using it."*

It is important to consciously note that you do not have to take people's advice. For many, other people's advice is worth what you paid for it — which in most cases is nothing. However, when you take advice, without truly discerning whether it is good or not, you are giving the design of your life away to someone else. What happens to your life when you allow someone else to design it for you rather than seek that for which you are truly called? What if you were told that you should be a doctor and the reality is that your true genius and desire lies in being a writer? You may end up being a fine doctor, help a lot of people and live financially secure. However, internally you will feel conflicted and unfulfilled. People will wonder why you could feel that way when you have "so much going for you..." Chances are you've got lots of Simon- recommended material things. Typically, they will next tell you how to "be." "You should be fulfilled and feel great with all that you have," they may likely say. So, now you have not only been told what to "do" but also how to "be!" By the end of your life, you will have done your best to fulfill the opinions of everyone else, but you never got to fulfill the Life Purpose that God himself designed for you.

> *It is important to consciously note that you do not have to take people's advice.*

Can you see why you may well look back on your life with an underlying emptiness as you never experienced the fulfillment of living out *your* life but that maybe of Simon's?

Some advice is not necessarily in the form of telling you what you should do but rather what you should not attempt to do. That is, they give you their perception of your abilities and will often steal the zest of an individual to go for a dream. Sometimes this is done innocently as they are simply trying to prevent you from "being hurt." Sometimes it is not so innocent as people are forced to look at themselves when you begin to excel and see they have no excuse. Many people would rather challenge you than look in the mirror and challenge themselves. Their feeling of inadequacy, however, is not your problem nor should it keep you from your potential that God desires to see you achieve. Marianne Williamson said, "Our deepest fear is not that we are inadequate. Our deepest fear is that we are powerful beyond measure. It is our light, not our darkness, that most frightens us. We ask ourselves, 'Who am I to be brilliant, gorgeous, talented, fabulous?' Actually, who are you not to be? You are a child of God. Your playing small does not serve the world. There is nothing enlightened about shrinking so that other people won't feel insecure around you. We are all meant to shine, as children do. We were born to make manifest the glory of God that is within us. It is not just in some of us; it is in everyone. And as we let our own light shine, we unconsciously give other people permission to do the same. As we are liberated from our own fear, our presence automatically liberates others."

Living inside-out says how about if you decide what your abilities are or are not. Thankfully, nobody stole the dream of Tyrone Curtis Bogues, better known as Muggsy Bogues.

He played for five teams during his 14-season career in the National Basketball Association (NBA) and was the shortest person to play in the NBA, standing at 5 feet 3 inches tall. Not possible? Obviously, he didn't realize that. "OK, a fluke," you say. Perhaps. But, then nobody told that to Earl Antoine Boykins. At 5 feet 5 inches, Boykins is the shortest active NBA player (at the time of this printing). Earl Boykins weighs only 133 pounds (60 kg) but according to various sources he can max-out on the bench press at 310 pounds. He is the shortest player in the history of the NBA to score over 30 points in a game — which he has reached several times, including a career-high 36 points. In 2003, he signed a five-year, $13.7-million deal with the Denver Nuggets.

Obviously, not all advice is bad. In fact, it is wise to pay for good advice from a mentor, consultant, or personal coach given they have the expertise and results in the subject matter. We will all become like those with whom we associate. Why? The people you associate with most you begin to think like. When you think like someone, you will make choices like them. When you make choices like them, you will end up like them — good or bad. G.I.G.O. — Garbage In, Garbage Out. Although originally a computer term, the concept is the same with your mind. When you let garbage into your mind, the quality of your decisions suffers. Poor decisions lead to poor consequences; i.e., garbage out. Just as you wouldn't let someone randomly dump garbage into your house, don't let them dump garbage into your mind. Carefully consider with whom you associate and certainly from whom you take advice. If

> *Just as you wouldn't let someone randomly dump garbage into your house, don't let them dump garbage into your mind.*

you want to hang out with the garbage man, don't be surprised if he dumps on you. Let the radar go up when someone suggests, "You should..." or "You can't..." Don't let it enter your mind with automatic acceptance. Evaluate it and the source it is coming from before you own it. Living inside-out is about letting your Life Purpose and the one who gave it to you direct you while freeing yourself from allowing other people to automatically direct you instead.

Freedom From Others: Button Pushers

I couldn't have been more than 14 years old when my friend yelled to me, "Watch this!" We exited the elevator inside a large hotel we were visiting with our families. "What?" I naively asked. People entered the elevator, the doors shut and he said, "Watch the numbers above the elevator doors — they'll stop on every number!" Sure enough the elevator did stop on every floor. My friend had hit every button in the elevator before getting off and the poor people inside were now experiencing the burden of my friend's sadistic humor. He loved to send people on his own personal journey; one floor at a time.

Button pushers exist in nearly everyone's life. You are having a fine day when that special someone shows up... "Not this time!" you tell yourself. Yet, before you know it, you feel your blood pressure rising along with a series of unpleasant emotions. It is as if you have buttons on your body that light you up emotionally and this person always seems to know just where they are. They push your buttons and you're off on an emotional journey.

The challenge is that, somewhere along the line, you have given others the permission to push your buttons. The reality is that nobody has buttons to push on you but rather they are able to get you to push your own buttons. Earlier in the book, we discussed that a person spitting on you doesn't really "make you mad," but rather only "makes you slimy wet." The manner by which you chose to process their action determines which emotional button you would internally push. It can be difficult to accept this principle at first but that is exactly why so few people have reached a high level of self-mastery.

Self-mastery can only occur when you take control back from others. Understand that although most everything can be taken from you, you will always have the ability to choose your attitude and assign meaning throughout life. Consequently, you can choose whose opinion you will value and what weight you will apply to another person's words. In addition, you can choose to look at everyone as a blessing in the sense that you can learn from everyone — some by their good example and some by their bad example. As the saying goes, "Everyone brightens the room, if not in the coming then at least in the going."

> *You can choose whose opinion you will value and what weight you will apply to another person's words.*

If you consider that you can learn something from everyone, then your button pusher must be one of your greatest teachers! From this individual, you will learn a lot about yourself; what you believe to be right and true, how to (or not to) treat others, and where you need to grow so that nobody has control over your emotions. Wow...that is a lot of information... apparently, your disturbing button pusher is a very valuable person in your life! Although it is obviously uncomfortable to learn about yourself, grow and take control through this process — it is transforming.

Once you have grown to the point that even the button pusher is not having an effect on you, then can you see how valuable that will be with respect to the rest of your life? Is it possible that the one area of personal growth and self-mastery that your button pusher is helping you with is exactly what you will need to fulfill your Life Purpose? Not only is it possible, put it is actually probable. There is a reason that you are easily emotional regarding certain topics or forms of treatment. It is meaningful to you for some reason. Discover why and you may find a connection with that for which you are being called. Master it and you may have found a great way to serve people.

FREEDOM FROM THE EGO:

The word "ego" comes directly from Latin and translates as "I myself." Therefore to have freedom from your ego translates into having freedom from yourself. This is truly your greatest freedom of all — it is the freedom which allows you to truly reinvent yourself. But, how is that possible to have freedom from yourself? It is possible when you understand who you truly are.

OK, will the real you please stand up? If I were to ask you, "Who are you?" what would be your response? Would you tell me your name? Would you tell me your occupation? Would you tell me your various roles as a parent, an organization leader, church leader, and so on? What would you say? The truth is most people have no idea who they are and, consequently, they relate who they ARE with what they DO. The byproduct of this is if the results in their life are good, then they are good. If the results are not good, then they are not good. Their state of BEING is completely conditional with the results of their DOING. This concept was introduced earlier in the book, but it is worthy to review as we look to reinvent ourselves. How do you modify something if you are unclear as to what it is in the first place?

> *The truth is most people have no idea who they are and, consequently, they relate who they ARE with what they DO.*

Who are you? You are a child of God. You were specifically designed with gifts, a purpose, and a mission to fulfill in life. You are amazing. You are special. How could you be anything else given the creator of the universe specifically designed and created you? Your parents may not have planned you, but God did. So remember, like an original masterpiece you are unique; just like everyone else. OK, that was just to lighten it up a bit but, as cliché as it may sound, it is true: you are the one and only you.

Yet, in addition to being a child of God that was specifically designed, taking it deeper, who are you? C.S. Lewis said, "You don't have a soul. You are a soul. You have a body." Similarly, remember you are not the talker in your head, that's Simon. You are the listener. You are not the one stating that, "I am ..." but rather you are the observer of such a statement. That is, the "True Self" (the observer) is not the same as the "Ego Self" (the talker). When you acknowledge the distinction and separation between the two, you will find great freedom.

The "True Self" is the real you. You are designed by your creator. You are about love, faith, intuition and rational thought. The True you seeks peace and purpose. The "Ego Self," on the other hand, is all about being right and winning. The Ego Self is prideful, self-centered, self-serving, and works off of emotional and fear-based thinking.

The Ego Self will fight consistently to be right and to win even if it means losing all sense of peace and purpose. Prior to acknowledging that you are not your Ego Self, you may naturally allow a fight to continue as the loss to the ego connects to a loss of one's self. Internally, you are not just fighting about a topic but rather you are fighting to maintain a sense of self. Fighting to maintain one's identity will never lead to peace and purpose. Pride is a false sense of self that is created by the ego. A prideful person has yet to discover their True Self. Rather, their world revolves selfishly around themselves (their Ego Self). Interestingly, even the letters in the words, "Pride" and "Sin" revolve around "I."

> *Once you understand that you don't necessarily need to allow your Ego Self to lead, that its defeat is not your defeat, then you are free to pursue what is best towards the fulfillment of your Life Purpose.*

Consequently, those who simply allow their lives to be led by their Ego Self are living destined to fight unnecessary battles and live with internal and external conflict. Once you understand that you don't necessarily need to allow your Ego Self to lead, that its defeat is not your defeat, then you are free to pursue what is best towards the fulfillment of your Life Purpose. Hence, the True Self is now leading. In other words, freedom from your Ego becomes possible simply by your acknowledgment of your separateness from it.

The real battle, therefore, is to be aware when your Ego Self is attempting to lead. It can be difficult to notice when it is happening. Society does a great job of telling us that we should stand up for this right or that one. Certainly, some of those rights are true to our values but many are simply Ego or prideful driven. Do you really need to go to the restaurant that you want verse the one your spouse wants? I know she always gets the one that she wants but does it really matter? Does it go against your core values to let her pick it? What about at the end of your life, will you wish you had fought harder all those years to win the choice of dinning locations? What it really comes down to is your ego telling you that, "She always gets to pick it; you deserve it this time. She's not respecting your wants! You need to stand up for yourself!" It gets you going and the next thing you realize, you are fighting for a feeling of respect and truly food is the furthest thing from the real core of the argument. This is not good. Your ego now has you fighting from pride attempting to force respect.

Your True Self values peace and is naturally inclined to serve others. The true you realizes that whether you eat enchiladas or grilled salmon really isn't going to be a life-changing decision. It isn't worthy of conflict and certainly doesn't need to trigger a prideful fight over respect.

With all of this said, anything can be taken to an unhealthy extreme. I not advocating that you don't share your opinions and become some sort of doormat with no voice whatsoever. That approach can lead to a codependent lifestyle where you completely lose yourself in someone else as you consume their wants and problems as one in the same as your own. At such a point, you really are not helping others by discarding yourself. In addition, I am not claiming that all pride is unhealthy. Pride within the context of recognition of accomplishment — a sense of pride regarding your work, family, or other activities and associations — can provide many healthy benefits and lead you to assume greater personal responsibility in your life.

What I am suggesting is that instead of engaging in conflict regularly, you first consider its source. Ask, "Am I fighting for my Ego self or my True self?" That is, is it ego driven or is it really something that conflicts with your core values and is not in alignment with your true self? If it's your Ego self, let it go; it doesn't hold real value. If it's for your True self, then stand strong to your values and stay the course. With this higher level of awareness and consideration, you now live a life true to who you are. You are not only able to let things go that don't matter as you understand that they are all about your ego, but you are also able to stand stronger than ever on the things that do matter as you understand that they are aligned with your True self.

The real battle in life, therefore, is to determine whether something is worthy of fighting for or not. The answer lies in the conflict's source — the Ego self or the True self. Free yourself from your ego by regularly acknowledging it and eliminating its influence over your choices. When you achieve this, you will be living true to yourself and in alignment with your Life Purpose. If success in life can be measured by the fulfillment of your Life Purpose, then success as a person can be measured by the degree to which you live according to your True self. By choosing to be a successful person, you are choosing to live at this higher level of consciousness — that is, living from the inside out, in alignment with your True self and free from the control of your ego.

FREEDOM TO REINVENT YOURSELF:

Once you realize that your past experiences don't need to hold you captive, that other people don't need to define you, and your ego doesn't need to direct you, then you are free to reinvent yourself. Not only is this healthy but it is absolutely necessary to grow and improve in order to become all that you were truly meant to be.

So, answer this pop-quiz: Today, compared to this time last year, are you "New & Improved" or are you the same model, just one year older? If you are not sure, then odds are you are the same model just older. To be "New & Improved" it takes thought and energy and not just a fresh coat of paint. You must creatively look at what parts to keep, what parts to discard, and what

> *Today, compared to this time last year, are you, "New & Improved" or are you the same model, just one year older?*

parts need improving. And, of course, it takes faith to move forward into anything new and unknown — even if we are certain that it is an improvement.

Being "New & Improved" is not going to happen by accident but rather by choice. In order for things to improve, you must choose to put forth the necessary thought and energy. Without them, the law of entropy says that things tend to become more disorganized and decay over time. Consider a car parked indefinitely. Does it begin to fall apart or look better? It falls apart, doesn't it? Conversely, you've never seen a bucket of bolts and scrap metal suddenly assemble itself into a car. That's obviously ridiculous. Yet, even as living creatures, we are no different — to improve, we must choose to improve.

If we want to be in better physical, spiritual or emotional shape we must choose to put forth thought and energy to make it so. Otherwise, over time we tend to gravitate towards being in worse physical, spiritual and emotional condition. In other words, we must choose to get better or, by default, we tend to get worse. Simply, we are not static creatures. We are very dynamic as we continue to age with each tick of the clock. Naturally over time, our bodies get older, our memories fade, our pants rise to our belly buttons and our ways become antiquated and more inflexible. We may even develop bitterness or resentment over events of our life. Consequently, avoid the default process by regularly choosing to put forth the thought and energy to get better!

Here is a plan to reinvent yourself:

1. Review, update and recommit to your Life Purpose Statement.

The first step of improvement always begins with reclarifying why you are here. What is God's will for your life? Your Life Purpose Statement answers this question. And, although your gifts, purpose, and core values are a part of your being and stay constant, the application of your gifts and purpose will develop like a fine wine over time. As we all age, our attention towards various facets of life naturally changes.

> *Although your gifts, purpose, and core values are a part of your being and stay constant, the application of your gifts and purpose will develop like a fine wine over time.*

For example, early in adulthood our attention may be wrapped around what job we should take or what cool car we should drive. Yet, over time, our attention may likely shift towards what is meaningful in life and eventually towards thoughts of leaving a legacy. In addition, we may have encountered a unique situation either in our own life or even in someone else's life that has grabbed our attention. That is, a death of a loved one, a divorce or a dramatic change in lifestyle can all lead to sudden changes of attention and perspective. As a result, it is essential that you regularly review and update your Life Purpose Statement.

Reinventing yourself is also about recommitting to your Life Purpose Statement. It is easy over time to drift away from maintaining a focus on what is truly important. Sometimes life can sidetrack us off our true assignment or off our commitment to holding strong to our values. In the business of life, and in our desire for

> *"God is the inventor of resurrection."*
> —Wes Beavis

short-term fulfillment, we may fall short of what we truly value long term. Perhaps, we feel discouraged by our past failures. It's time to bounce back. Perhaps, we feel it's too late. It's not. As author Wes Beavis says, "God is the inventor of resurrection." It's time to recommit to centering your life around your Life Purpose and the one who gave it to you. Recommit to living a life not by accident but on purpose. Tell Simon what you're going to do.

2. Recreate your Wheel of Life.

The next step of improvement is to reclarify where you are in your life. Your life is like a movie rolling along through time. Taking inventory of the present requires stopping for a moment and viewing the current slide of the film. In other words, it's time for a "reality check."

How true is your Wheel of Life? How has it changed? Reinventing yourself includes re-prioritizing various areas in your life. If necessary, consider using the "Tournament of Priorities" to gain clarity. With this understanding, write down specifically what adjustments can be made to improve the trueness of your life?

3. Get personal with yourself.

Now, it is time to really get personal. What areas of you need improvement? Be real. Remember, the 11th Commandment: "Thou shall not fake thyself out." How can you really adjust and update yourself if you are not in tune with reality? Gain clarity by answering the following questions:

• What are my faults? This question is about being real with yourself. During the development of your Life Purpose Statement, you already acknowledged your gifts and talents. Now it is time to admit and list your faults (and we're not talking about hair problems). This process will do two things: First, it will give you clarity on personal areas to be aware of and to improve on. Secondly, it will help you focus less on others' faults as you are now focused on your own. This is a Biblical principle; to focus on your own faults rather than those of others. Christ said, "And why worry about a speck in your friend's eye when you have a log in your own? How can you think of saying, 'Let me help you get rid of that speck in your eye,' when you can't see past the log in your own eye." (Matthew 7:3-4) After admitting and listing your faults, note the most important ones to work on improving immediately.

- What do I need to let go? Can you imagine a captain of a boat saying, "We need more power!" while dragging an anchor around? It would be even more ridiculous if he was aware of his anchor and continued dragging it anyway; mutiny might be an option here. The question here refers to your personal anchors. What are you dragging around? Have you made mistakes? Did you miss an opportunity? Did you do someone wrong? Make a note of any anchors you have. Note the lesson from each of them. Acknowledge whether there is anything you can do to bring closure to them. If so, do it. If not, then...ready...let it go! It is over. It is done. Cut the anchor chain and allow yourself the freedom to sail your personal ocean of life.

- What is it like to be on the other side of me? Ask this question to someone whom you trust, respect, and who knows you well. Their answer may be eye-opening. Others' perspectives of you may reveal possible personal blind spots. You may be very surprised by what you learn. Truth seekers are excited about such a possibility. They love the idea of learning something about themselves that they were unaware of and can improve upon. This knowledge can be the basis for a great reinventing of one's self. However, the fragile individual who truly doesn't seek truth but rather momentary comfort will avoid this question like the plague. They would rather avoid any discomfort that may arise by such a new perspective, than seek the beauty of life that unfolds by their adjustment to it. Be a truth-seeker, take a deep breath and ask the question. Then, consider their perspective as your look to reinvent yourself.

4. Get personal with others.

Life is about relationships. We are relational beings and are designed to interact with others. The more you develop positive relationships, the healthier your life will become. Cherish those in your life that truly love you and care for you. Protect and invest into those relationships. On the other hand, be aware of toxic relationships. Adjust or bring closure to those relationships. Ask these two questions:

• Who do I need to forgive? One of the most important things that you can do to reinvent yourself is to forgive others. Hanging onto the pain caused by another only hurts you. Bitterness and resentment freely grow where forgiveness doesn't exist. As discussed earlier, if you can't forgive them for their sake than at least do it for your own. Forgiving someone doesn't mean that you must trust them, like them, or even forget what they did. Rather, it simply means that you forgive them. If they have asked for your forgiveness then let them know that you forgive them. If they have not asked for your forgiveness then let God know that you forgive them. For most people, leaning on God's grace is required to truly forgive. Determine who it is that you need to forgive, and forgive them.

- Who do I need to appreciate? Just as it is important to acknowledge and forgive those who have hurt you most, it is also important to acknowledge and appreciate those who you value most. Sharing your gratitude towards another person is life transforming as you connect heart to heart with them. It is essential that reinventing yourself includes establishing deeper relationships with the people you value most. Many people may have no idea how valuable they are to you. You will probably be surprised. Who are the significant people in your life? If only 10 people could remain in your world, who would they be? Now, let these people know it. Share with them how important they are to you and be specific as to why. If you were on your death bed, what would you say to them? Say it now!

5. Live like you were dying.

The final step of reinventing yourself is to give life everything you've got. Although the words, "Live like you were dying," may initially seem a bit depressing, the opposite is actually true. If you knew that you were dying, an undeniable clarity of personal priorities would quickly come into focus along with an urgency to do something about them. Carpe Diem! Live life with such passion as to make every moment count! As the saying goes, "Life is not a journey to the grave with the intention of arriving safely in a pretty and well-preserved body, but rather to skid in broadside, thoroughly used up, totally worn out, and proclaiming, 'Wow, what a ride!!!'" Re-invent yourself to live like you were dying but don't kill yourself...Let the transformation begin!

Check

Box   Reinvent Yourself — Summary to do list:

	Review, update and re-commit to your Life Purpose Statement.
	Commit to centering your life around your Life Purpose and the one who gave it to you.
	Re-create your Wheel of Life.
	Write down specifically what adjustments can be made to improve the trueness of your life?
	Admit and list your faults. Note the most important ones to work on improving immediately.
	Make a note of any anchors you have. Allow yourself freedom from them.
	Ask, "What is it like to be on the other side of me?" Consider their perspective.
	Determine who it is that you need to forgive, and forgive them.
	Determine who are the significant people in your life, and share your appreciation with them.
	Commit to living like you were dying!

CHAPTER 23

Making a Difference

*There are two types of people who will tell you that you
cannot make a difference in this world: Those who are
afraid to try and those who are afraid you will succeed.*
–Ray Goforth

Your Life Purpose is always connected to other people as
you apply your gifts and purpose, follow your passions and
live by your values. Therefore, the more inspired your life,
the more on purpose you live, the greater impact you will
have on others. Whether it is taking a stand for that which
holds true to your values as did Martin Luther King, Jr. with
human rights or whether it is dedicating your life to the application of your purpose as did Mother Teresa with serving
the poor and helpless, living your life according to your Life
Purpose will positively impact other people. Specifically, your
inspired or "in-spirit" life will make a difference with others
through your love, service and by being an example.

The connectivity of living a life according to your Life Purpose and providing love, service and being an example to others is so interwoven that it works in both directions. That is,
not only are these blessings a direct byproduct of living on
purpose, but by looking for opportunities to pass them on,
you may actually further clarify your Life Purpose. For ex-

ample, find a way to serve others and in the process you may likely discover unrealized personal gifts and passions that lead to your ultimate Life Purpose.

Sometimes there isn't too much of a good thing — you don't often hear people at the end of their life saying, "I just loved people too much, I served others too often and I was too good of an example living by my core values." No, rather these individuals are more likely to hear their creator say, "Well done my good and faithful servant."

CHAPTER 24

Love Others

There are many in the world who are dying for a piece of bread,
but there are many more dying for a little love.
−Mother Teresa

It's been said that people really need to know two things — that they are loved and that everything is going to be alright.

> *People really need to know two things—that they are loved and that everything is going to be alright.*

This really boils down to love and hope. Isn't it amazing how the most valuable things that we can give another person are free? Even more remarkable is the fact that we don't have a limited supply to give. It's not like you are going to run out of love or encouragement because you just gave the last of it to the previous person. You may not want to love and encourage, you may be afraid to love and encourage, but the resources are there. Christ not only believed that it is important to love but he commanded it as he said, "Love the Lord your God with all your heart and with all your soul and with all your mind. This is the first and greatest commandment." And the second is like it: "Love your neighbor as yourself." Christ was the epitome of God's love and spent his ministry sharing the "Good News" of love and hope.

In order to truly pass on love to our "neighbor" we must leave our comfort zone and move into our compassion zone. Have you ever noticed a homeless person but kept walking? It's uncomfortable to stop and engage in dialogue, isn't it? However, you may be the only person compassionate enough to pass on some love and hope. Can you take a moment to share love and give hope to

> *In order to truly pass on love to our 'neighbor' we must leave our comfort zone and move into our compassion zone.*

another human being or are you really too busy with more important things to do? Are they not worthy of it from you? Don't let your ego answer that! Remember, "There but by the grace of God go I."

If someone offered to give you a $20 bill, you would consider that a kind gift with an obvious value, wouldn't you? What if they crumpled it up before handing it to you? Would you look at it in its crumpled state and say that you didn't want it now because it has lost its value? Of course not. That would be ridiculous. You know perfectly well that its value is in what it is and not in its momentary condition. You may feel inclined to straighten it up a bit but regardless its value has not changed. People are the same way. Although someone may appear to be crumpled up by their life experiences, their value has not changed. They are still a priceless child of God and worthy of our attention.

Perhaps a person doesn't deserve your love because of their actions. It is possible. I won't debate that. However, I'm encouraging you to follow Christ's commandment to love your neighbor anyway. After all, God still loves you in spite of your sin.

> *Love others because of your character, not because of their conduct.*

Love others because of your character, not because of their conduct. For most people, this puts a very different and challenging perspective on the concept of love. Now, loving others is based on who you are rather than on what they've done.

I know this perspective directly opposes what Simon says you should do. Your ego is screaming to give them what's coming to them! However, love says rather than giving them what they deserve, give them what they need. Do they need grace? Do they need to be heard? Do they need help? Since there is an endless list of possible needs, this means love is now taking it further by directing you to seek to understand them. Yes, truly loving others requires emotional and spiritual maturity.

> *Love says rather than giving them what they deserve, give them what they need.*

The Bible shares an amazing story about a woman that the teachers of religious law and Pharisees brought that they had caught in the act of adultery. They put her in front of the crowd to whom Jesus was speaking and noted that the Law of Moses says to stone her. Then, they asked Jesus what he would do? They were trying to trap him into saying something they could use against him. If he said not to stone her, then he was contradicting the Law of Moses. If he suggested that she be stoned, then he was in alignment with the Law of Moses but contradicting his own non-violent teachings.

The religious leaders and Pharisees kept demanding an answer, so Jesus finally stood up and said, "All right, stone her. But let those who have never sinned throw the first stones!" When the accusers heard this, they slipped away one by one, beginning with the oldest, until only Jesus was left in the middle of the crowd with the woman. Then he said to her, "Woman, where are your accusers? Didn't even one of them condemn you?" "No Lord!" she said. And Jesus said, "Neither do I. Go and sin no more." (John 8:3-11)

Loving someone certainly doesn't mean that you have to agree with their choices nor does it require you to stand by idle or turn a blind eye to that which you know to be wrong. In fact, nothing could be further from the truth. However, to again reference a quote by Martin Luther King, Jr., "He who you will change, you must first love." Jesus showed God's grace to the woman, loved her and then instructed her to change her ways.

Choose to live in the compassion zone where you will truly experience life's greatest gifts. Send your ego on a permanent vacation and see what miracles unfold as you love others rather than ignore, judge or condemn them.

What does Love mean?

"When my grandmother got arthritis, she couldn't bend over and paint her toenails anymore. So my grandfather does it for her all the time, even when his hands got arthritis too. That's love."
Rebecca- age 8

"When someone loves you, the way they say your name is different. You just know that your name is safe in their mouth."
Billy - age 4

"Love is when a girl puts on perfume and a boy puts on shaving cologne and they go out and smell each other."
Karl - age 5

"Love is what makes you smile when you're tired."
Terri - age 4

"Love is when my mommy makes coffee for my daddy and she takes a sip before giving it to him, to make sure the taste is OK."
Danny - age 7

"Love is when you kiss all the time. Then when you get tired of kissing, you still want to be together and you talk more. My Mommy and Daddy are like that. They look gross when they kiss"
Emily - age 8

"Love is what's in the room with you at Christmas if you stop opening presents and listen."
Bobby - age 7

"Love is when you tell a guy you like his shirt, then he wears it everyday."
Noelle - age 7

"Love is like a little old woman and a little old man who are still friends even after they know each other so well."
Tommy - age 6

"During my piano recital, I was on a stage and I was scared.
I looked at all the people watching me and saw my daddy
waving and smiling. He was the only one doing that.
I wasn't scared anymore."
Cindy - age 8

"Love is when Mommy gives Daddy the best
piece of chicken."
Elaine-age 5

"Love is when Mommy sees Daddy smelly and sweaty and
still says he is handsomer than Robert Redford."
Chris - age 7

"Love is when your puppy licks your face even after you
left him alone all day."
Mary Ann - age 4

"When you love somebody, your eyelashes go up and down
and little stars come out of you."
Karen - age 7

And the final one — author and lecturer Leo Buscaglia
once talked about a contest he was asked to judge. The
purpose of the contest was to find the most caring child.
The winner was a 4-year-old child whose next-door neighbor
was an elderly gentleman who had recently lost his wife.
Upon seeing the man cry, the little boy went into the old
gentleman's yard, climbed onto his lap, and just sat there.
When his mother asked what he had said to the neighbor,
the little boy said, "Nothing, I just helped him cry."

-Anonymous

CHAPTER 25

Serve Others

The true meaning of life is to plant trees, under whose shade
you do not expect to sit.
–Nelson Henderson

There is an old saying, "Life is like tennis. The one who serves the most seldom loses!" It's easy to say but often our ego leads us to fall back and "look out for No. 1." Ironically, however, "No. 1" truly wins only through the service of others. As Sir Winston Churchill said, "We make a living by what we get, but we make a life by what we give."

Now, certainly serving others can be taken to an extreme where you have completely lost touch with your individual needs; you literally serve others to your own demise. I am not suggesting such an approach. Even the flight attendant (good Simon) says, "Secure your own mask first and then secure those of your children." Good advice since if you're passed out, it is hard to serve others! However, given that you've applied this airline safety principle to your life and your basic needs are met,

> *When you consider that your assignment (or calling) in life is the application of your purpose to your passion, then service to others is the automatic by-product of living an inspired life.*

then your primary focus in life can be serving the needs of others.

When you consider that your assignment (or calling) in life is the application of your purpose to your passion, then service to others is the automatic byproduct of living an inspired life. That is, the fulfillment of your Life Purpose automatically and specifically includes the serving of other people.

In early 2000, Catherine Ryan Hyde released a book entitled, "Pay It Forward." The book stemmed from an incident in her life some 20 years earlier. She was driving alone at night in a rough area of Los Angeles. As she exited the freeway, suddenly her car's engine stopped, all of its lights went out, and the passenger compartment began filling with smoke. She pulled over and as she got out of the car, two men came running towards her with a blanket. She had no idea what was happening and initially thought the worst of the approaching men. Then, one man popped the hood of her car. The engine was on fire with flames burning along the throttle line. He immediately proceeded to smother the blaze with his blanket. The fire department quickly arrived but the fire was already out. Once it was all over, she looked to thank the two men but they were gone.

It was over the course of the following months that she decided if she couldn't pay someone back, she certainly could pay it forward. The result of her simple desire to serve someone led to her authoring a book. The concept was simple. What if you did a favor for three people and instead of being paid back they, in return, did a favor for three different people, and so on? What would happen? The idea was to change the world one favor at a time. Her concept led to a calling and Warner Brother's released a movie based on the book. Her

"Pay it Forward Movement" has since captured the hearts of people all over the world.

Imagine if Catherine Ryan Hyde hadn't followed her natural instinct to serve. She wouldn't have discovered a personal calling and millions of lives around the world wouldn't have been blessed.

So what do you do if your car hasn't recently caught fire leading you to write a book and so on? Where do you begin to serve? Often, I find people are open to making a difference by serving others but simply aren't sure where to begin or what to do. The solution, according to Billy Zeoli, is simple.

Zeoli, the founder and current president of Gospel Communications, Inc., was a close friend and spiritual advisor to President Ford. He was well connected internationally in the political world and had significant influence on some of the most well-known sports figures in America. In fact, the list of people worldwide that he has met and positively impacted is truly mind boggling. I asked him what he found was the secret to making a difference in this world. He said to simply, "be available."

> *"When people pray, 'God, I'm available... let me be a tool to serve your will,' amazing things happen."*
> —Billy Zeoli

He said that when people pray, "God, I'm available...let me be a tool to serve your will," amazing things happen.

He reminded me how most people are too busy serving their own agenda to be concerned with anyone else's, let alone God's agenda. Yet, ironically, if you switch that around and seek to serve others by seeking to serve God's will, your life will be transformed and your Life Purpose will be fulfilled.

For many people it takes a traumatic event in their life to

slow down, tune out the incessant Simon chatter and finally tune into the quiet whisper from within. It is this moment where one begins to connect with God's will rather than running on Simon's lifelong personal agenda. It happened to me, to Catherine Ryan Hyde, and it is believed to have happened to Albert Nobel.

> *For many people it takes a traumatic event in their life to slow down, tune-out the incessant Simon chatter and finally tune into the quiet whisper from within.*

In 1888, a French newspaper erroneously published Nobel's obituary in an act of confusion with the actual death of his brother, Ludvig. Albert was best known in his day as the inventor of dynamite. As a poet and pacifist, he had intended his invention to be used for peaceful purposes and was dismayed by its significant use as a powerful instrument of war. When the obituary ran, the newspaper condemned Albert for his invention with the headline, "Le marchand de la mort est mort" (the merchant of death is dead). It further went on to say, "Dr. Alfred Nobel, who became rich by finding ways to kill more people faster than ever before, died yesterday." In an attempt to redeem his reputation and to promote his deeply imbedded desire for peace, Albert Nobel established the Nobel Prize for outstanding achievements in the fields of physics, chemistry, physiology or medicine, literature, and the promotion of world peace.

CHAPTER 26

Be an Example

A good example is the best sermon.
–Benjamin Franklin

The world can never have too many examples of people who stand firm with their core values, apply their purpose, and seek to fulfill their assignment in life. There is nothing more powerful than a person's example. John Quincy Adams, the 6th US President, said, "If your actions inspire others to dream more, learn more, do more and become more, you are a leader." In other words, stop doing what Simon says, live your Life Purpose and consequently lead others to discover, pursue and fulfill their Life Purpose as well.

> *The world can never have too many examples of people who stand firm with their core values, apply their purpose, and seek to fulfill their assignment in life.*

Both of my parents are wonderful examples of people who live firmly by their core values. Not only did they teach me solid principles and the concept of core values, but they showed me through their example how to truly live by them even when difficult situations arise.

Let me share an event from my life that occurred in 1977.

My mother had taught me to swim and now at the age of 10 I was a focused little boy attempting to win the high-point award at the Woodlands Swimming Invitational. At this year-end competition, all of the local swim clubs came together and each swimmer swam one or two events. The one with the two best races would win the age group high-point trophy. I was so excited knowing that I had a good chance at it. I won my first event and all I needed to do was win my second one. It was the 50-yard freestyle. My rival had also won his first event and the duel was on in this final race. The two of us competed and, when we finished, I looked up and saw the timers post the same time for both of us. We had tied! Consequently, it came down to the three judges to decide the winner. They sat at the end of the pool just by the water's edge and one at a time they held up a card with the lane number of the swimmer they felt had won. The first judge awarded it to me. The second judge awarded it to my rival. I remember anxiously looking at the third judge while still hanging on the lane line in the pool. There was a pause and then there it was: The third judge held up a card with my rival's lane number on it. "It can't be!" I thought to myself. My rival had won and the most difficult part to swallow was that the third judge...was my mother!

That night at home, I asked her why she had voted for him. She then explained that she voted for the other boy because she truly believed that she saw him touch first and that she had to tell the truth. "Although nobody would have even known if I had not told the truth, I would have known," she said. I remember understanding the lesson but, at the time, still wished I was enjoying the victory.

Two weeks later, however, we traveled to the final event

of the season — the County Championships. There my rival and I were on again. This time, more determined than ever after not winning the invitational, I won both events. I won the high-point award and it was presented by a swimming hero of mine at the time, 1976 four-time Olympic gold medalist John Naber. We took a photo together and I was one happy 10-year-old.

As I reflect back on that experience, I realize that had my mother falsely awarded me the victory at the invitational, I may not have had the focus to win the championships. How true is it that if we claim something that isn't real, we may well miss the true victory.

More importantly, however, I appreciate my mother's commitment towards actually standing on her principles and core values. As the old saying by Ralph Waldo Emerson goes, "What you do speaks so loudly that I cannot hear what you say." She didn't just talk about honesty, she modeled it to me. I can only imagine how her heart must have sunk when she realized it was all coming down to her call. With all eyes on her and her son's hopes in her hands, she had quite a decision to make. She could have chosen to provide a short-term celebration. Instead, she chose to provide a long-term example that I've since applied in my life, leading to many of my life's true high points. Her willingness to value honesty and be an example to me was the true award I received that season.

But what if you haven't been such a great example up to this point in your life? It's never too late to begin. In fact, sometimes setting a new good example can have a dramatic effect as people can clearly see a decided change. Consider the following two historical stories:

The day was Feb. 20, 1942 and World War II was raging. A group of American fighter pilots took off from their ships in the South Pacific for a mission. One of the pilots was Lt. Commander Butch O'Hare. After taking off, he noticed that someone had forgotten to top off his fuel and he needed to return to the ship as he wouldn't have the needed fuel otherwise. Upon returning back, he unexpectedly ran into a squadron of Japanese bombers headed directly towards the fleet of ships. Given the fighter pilots were away, the ships were left unprotected. Without being able to warn the ships, he decided that he had to do something himself. He dove into the squadron of Japanese planes with his wing mounted guns firing off rounds. He took out a few surprised planes and, after he ran out of ammunition, continued his attack by attempting to clip off the other planes' tail or a wing. Finally, the Japanese squadron diverted their course. O'Hare then flew his badly damaged plane back to the ships.

His solo attack was caught on film on the camera mounted on his plane and it could be seen that he had single handedly destroyed five enemy planes and protected the American fleet. For his bravery, he was later awarded the first Navy's ace of WWII and the first Naval Aviator to win the Congressional Medal of Honor. Today, the O'Hare airport in Chicago is named after this courageous man.

A number of years earlier is the story of another man, known as Easy Eddie. He lived in Chicago and worked directly for Al Capone as his attorney. Easy

Eddie was an exceptional attorney and able to keep Capone out of jail for years. Although his work gained him great fortune through Capone, it was far from respectful. Capone was free to continue his horrific criminal activities. Easy Eddie cared primarily about one thing — his son. He gave his son the best of every-thing...the best lifestyle, the best education, and the best opportunities. However, he could not give his son a good name or a good example. Money alone doesn't buy either. As a result, he made a difficult decision that he knew would cost him dearly. He decided to testify against Capone and the Mob. Although there remains somewhat of a lingering debate as to why exactly he would turn to such good after such a long history of bad, experts agree that, particularly given his obvious fate, only love for his son could lead to such a decision. His testimony was significant and contributed to the conviction of Capone. Within a year, he was gunned down and killed but at least he left an example for his son.

What do the two stories have in common? Easy Eddie was Butch O'Hare's father. Perhaps Easy Eddie's final decision in the end to do right in spite of most certainly fatal consequences was the example that O'Hare needed to take the courageous path that he did.

> *If you have not been the example to others that you know you could be, decide today to begin it.*

If you have not been the example to others that you know you can be, decide today to begin it. The past is over. Put it in the history books. You may have a family history of not setting the right example; a process repeated generation after generation. At some point, someone needs to break the chain. If so, let that person be you and let the time be now! Set a new course of history. Embrace your past, learn from it, and let it go. Start setting the right example now. Live by your core values. Let them guide your decision making. Define your purpose and apply it to all areas of your life. Then, recognize your passions and go after them! Let your life completely reflect who you are and what you are about. Set sail on your Life Purpose and let the world know you by it. Leave Simon behind; he's old news.

> *Let your life completely reflect who you are and what you are about.*

Conclusion

As the saying goes, "Today is the first day of the rest of your life." Whether your life to this point has been wonderful, average, or something out of a bad movie, how about deciding today to make it nothing less than spectacular?! Let's face it, you're still on earth occupying space and breathing for a reason: to fulfill your Life Purpose. It's your life mission. Did you define it or has Simon? Turn back into the pages of this book and crystallize your Life Purpose. Let it inspire you! Life wasn't meant to be lived simply by accident. It was meant to be lived creatively and on purpose!

You already know your birthday; the day you were introduced into the world. Let today be your Purpose Day: the day the world sees and experiences the real you. Shine not because of how the world reflects upon you, but because of whom you are. In Mother Teresa's children's home in Calcutta, the following words are displayed on the wall:

ANYWAY

People are unreasonable, illogical, and self-centered,
LOVE THEM ANYWAY
If you do good, people will accuse you of
selfish, ulterior motives,
DO GOOD ANYWAY
If you are successful,
you win false friends and true enemies,
SUCCEED ANYWAY
The good you do will be forgotten tomorrow,
DO GOOD ANYWAY
Honesty and frankness make you vulnerable,
BE HONEST AND FRANK ANYWAY
What you spent years building may be
destroyed overnight,
BUILD ANYWAY
People really need help
but may attack you if you help them,
HELP PEOPLE ANYWAY
Give the world the best you have
And you'll get kicked in the teeth,
GIVE THE WORLD THE BEST YOU'VE GOT ANYWAY.

Commandments attributed to Kent M. Keith
(c) Copyright Kent M. Keith 1968, renewed 2001

Remember, in the final analysis, it is between you and God. It was never between you and them anyway.

May God bless you as you bless others with your purpose and through the pursuit of your passions. Live your life and not Simon's. Live it big; supersize it! Live it beginning right now focused on your Life Purpose! And, live it so the defining words regarding your life are a confident "Mission Accomplished." And finally, as a last resort for those still listening to Simon, Simon says, "Go live your Life Purpose!"

Begin your inspired life today by joining others in a Simon Says Revolution! Be a part of the movement. Make a difference in your life and in the lives of others. Check out what it's all about at: www.SimonSaysRevolution.com

Notes

Chp 2: Every birth comes with a purpose
Winston Churchill quote – From the book: *Churchill* by Martin Gilbert

Chp 5: You are a solution to someone
Norman Ernest Borlaug complete story – adapted from site: http://www.campsilos.org/mod4/s1a.shtml

Chp 8: Anger is a clue …
Rosa Parks quote – From the book--Rosa Parks: *My Story* (Haskins and Parks, 1992)

Martin Luther King history portion - *Dissent Magazine*, Winter 2006, Peter Dreier

Chp 10: Establishing where you are
Create a wheel of life - adapted from *Finding Your Purpose*, Barbara Braham, p.14

Chp 11: Creating your life purpose statement
Personal Mission Statement (steps 1 – 3) – adapted from

internet article: http://www.revolutionhealth.com/healthy-living/relationships/time/time-savers/life-goals

by Laura Stack

Purpose Statement (steps 1 – 3) – adapted from, *Are you using your Genius at work,* Dick Richards

Chp 14: Are your core values real

"Shoulds" concept – adapted from *Finding Your Purpose,* Barbara Braham, p.46

Chp 16: Emotional intelligence

The Cookie Thief by Valerie Cox— *Chicken Soup for the Soul,* (c) 1996 by Jack Canfield and Mark Victor Hansen Reprinted with the permission of Health Communications, Inc., http://www.hcibooks.com/

Chp 17: Attitude

Attitude: Possibility Thinking – Story on George Dantzig quoting from article on web: http://www-history.mcs.standrews.ac.uk/Biographies/Dantzig_George.html

Chp 18: Actions

Establishing Priorities – Priorities Tournament Section -- adapted from *The On-purpose Person,* McCarthy

Focus – Jim Carey story of check—Source: website: http://www.intouchmag.com/visualization.html

Willpower—adapted from article on website: http://www.stevepavlina.com/blog/2005/06/self-discipline-willpower/ by Steve Pavlina

Review--Review the Results—Story of Henry Cloud teaching—from his book, *Integrity*, p159

Review--Review the Results—Baseball's Top 100 strikeout list reference—http://en.wikipedia.org/wiki/List_of_Top_100_all-time_Major_League_Baseball_strikeout_leaders

Chp 22: Freedom
Freedom From Others: Advice Givers—Info on Tyrone Curtis Bogues: Site- http://en.wikipedia.org/wiki/Muggsy_Bogues

Freedom From Others: Advice Givers—Info on Earl Antoine Boykins: Site- http://en.wikipedia.org/wiki/Earl_Boykins

Chp 25: Serve others
Catherine Ryan Hyde story facts from an interview posted on the site: http://www.randomhouse.com/vintage/catalog/display.pperl?isbn=978030

Nobel story facts from site: http://en.wikipedia.org/wiki/Alfred_Nobel

Chp 26: Be an example
Butch O'Hare & Easy Eddie story: Facts from site: http://www.snopes.com/glurge/ohare.asp & from site: http://www.truthorfiction.com/rumors/b/butchandeddie.htm